House Doctor

A-Z OF DESIGN

Collins

House Doctor
A-Z OF DESIGN

ann maurice

First published in Great Britain in 2005 by
Collins, an imprint of
HarperCollins*Publishers*
77–85 Fulham Palace Road
London W6 8JB

The Collins website address is **www.collins.co.uk**

Collins is a registered trademark of HarperCollins*Publishers* Ltd.

Some of the material in this book originally appeared in the
House Doctor books by Ann Maurice with Fanny Blake.

Project editor: Stuart Cooper for Essential Works
Designer: Mark Stevens for Essential Works
Copy editor: Phil Hunt for Essential Works
Additional text: Michael Jones

10 9 8 7 6 5 4 3 2 1

The author and publishers have made every reasonable effort to contact
all copyright holders. Any errors that may have occurred are inadvertent
and anyone who for any reason has not been contacted is invited to write
to the publishers so that full acknowledgement may be made in subsequent
editions of this work.

A catalogue record for this book is available from the British Library

ISBN 0 00 720078 1

Printed and bound in Great Britain by the Bath Press Ltd

CONTENTS

INTRODUCTION

It seems like just yesterday that I was invited to Britain to introduce the concept of home staging on national television. Today, nine years later, the success of the House Doctor series (now in its seventh year) continues to amaze me. Its success, I believe, can be attributed to many things, but mostly to the fact that in every programme there is something that the viewer can take on board to make their home look or feel just a little bit better.

The new 16-part series *House Doctor A–Z of Design* is a compilation of some of the best tips featured on the programme over the years in a unique and entertaining format. It is filled with clips from the seven years of programming (some never before seen on television), with a running commentary that is witty as well as informative. And for all you avid House Doctor fans out there, it's a real stroll down memory lane.

I am happy to present you with this latest book, *House Doctor A–Z of Design*, which is not only meant to be a companion to the series, but a source of inspiration and advice for anyone who is interested in improving their home. This book is a complete and easy-to- follow A–Z guide that looks at every imaginable household dilemma and provides practical and viable solutions. It contains numerous real-life case studies and before-and-after transformations, which clearly demonstrate my House Doctor philosophy in every detail. Although much of the advice in the book will be useful to those who are preparing their homes for sale, the ideas and design principles presented here can be universally applied to any living situation.

What I appreciate most about *House Doctor A–Z of Design* is that it is a serious book that does not take itself too seriously. Although it's packed with useful information, transformational tips and design direction, the book is written in a lighthearted style. Design is a serious business, but it should be an enjoyable experience as well. My hope is that while you are learning from reading this book, you will also take the time to pause and have a few laughs on me. Enjoy!

AMBIENCE

There are various ways of creating a relaxed atmosphere in a home. The most obvious method is to use lighting to enhance the mood, but you must also think about other elements such as colour, texture and smell. If you are redesigning the room for yourself, you can add any number of personal touches to create an ambience that suits you. If, however, you are staging your house – presenting your property for sale – you will have to work a bit harder and make your home seem the most desirable property in the area.

DOCTOR'S ORDERS

- Eliminate any unpleasant smells by opening windows.
- Scented candles, a drop or two of vanilla essence on a light bulb or a stick of cinnamon in a warm oven smell delicious.
- Pot-pourri in the living room and a bowl of lemons in the dining room or kitchen look attractive and will counter any odours.
- The smells of baking bread and freshly brewed coffee are notoriously seductive when it comes to showing off your home.
- Play soft music, but nothing that jars.
- Healthy green-leaved plants refresh and contribute a sense of well-being.
- Fresh flowers add colour and fragrance to a room.

SETTING THE SCENE

When staging a home, the ideal ambience to aim for is one that leaves your potential buyers believing that your property is the only house for them. Of course presenting them with an attractive home that looks as if it can be moved into without any work being done to it is essential. But there are various subliminal suggestions that you can offer that will make the place seem even more attractive.

The game is to play with your buyers' senses so that you hook them into feeling comfortable. Imagine how you can make a subtle appeal to each of the five senses: sight, hearing, taste, smell, touch. Each room should be looking its best – clean, tidy, but lived in. If it's the evening, remember to turn the lights on so rooms are at their most inviting. Arrange the lights to emphasize the best features. A decoratively laid table can offer a subliminal invitation to anyone who enters. Soft music could be playing in the background. Flowers and plants help clear the air and give a feeling of life.

Most effective of all can be the addition of pleasant smells. After all, no one enjoys the smell of yesterday's cooking, damp washing, cigarette smoke or pets. And don't worry about how much effort you put into staging – your buyer will only remember the general welcoming atmosphere of the house, not the individual tricks you have used to seduce them.

LEFT Small tableaux such as this simple arrangement of flowers, candles and fruit will create instant atmosphere.

BELOW Whether redesigning for yourself or preparing for a sale, creating the right mood needs careful thought. Clear away any clutter and make sure your plants are well watered. Straighten sofas and plump up cushions. The whole room should create a feeling of welcome and comfort.

ANTIQUES

When it comes to adding atmosphere to a room a few carefully chosen antiques can be just what the doctor ordered; the problem with you Brits is you just don't know when to stop. There's no shortage of antiques in British homes, quite the opposite in fact – too many of your houses are marred by that knick-knack nightmare, antique overload. Antiques can be beautiful accessories; the trick is knowing how to display them to your advantage. Choose just a few of your favourite things and take a hammer to the rest – auction them off. Make sure shelving isn't cluttered – give those choice items plenty of space or they'll crowd the room and lose their impact. Highlight your antiques through clever lighting or the natural framing of an alcove, for example. Most important of all, don't be an antique addict – curb that clutter and remember, less is more.

DOCTOR'S ORDERS

- **Display just a few choice items from your collection.**
- **Rotate large collections so that each piece can be fully appreciated.**
- **Tie areas together by displaying large collections across different rooms.**
- **Utilize lighting to emphasize key pieces.**
- **Limit the amount of items on shelves to give the impression of space.**
- **Sell unwanted or unusable items at an auction or donate them to a local charity shop.**

CASE NOTES: CURING AN ADDICTION

The owner of this house loved antique collecting to the extent that she was being crowded out of her own home. When I walked into the dining room, I felt dizzy with the effect of all the things crammed in there. This woman had to be stopped.

We had to be brutal about what was kept and what went into storage before we could show off the size of the room and its principal features. I had to persuade the owner to sell, chuck out or store many of her beloved antiques. Strictly limiting the number of items on shelves allows each one to be seen and appreciated, and gives an impression of space. With this in mind, I told the owner that she could only have six things displayed on the dresser. Initially, she had to be stopped from sneaking out more but eventually admitted that she felt liberated by decluttering herself so radically.

With the jumble edited right down on either side and a single picture on the mantel shelf, the fireplace became the rightful focal point. Removing the tablecloth and clutter also meant that the furniture could be properly seen and admired. When we'd finished, the room appeared much lighter, airier and more inviting. And hopefully the owner's antique addiction was cured for good!

before

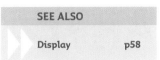

SEE ALSO

Display   p58

after

A

APPEARANCE

Whether you're selling a home or living in it, appearances are all-important. You never get a second chance to make a first impression, so make sure you get it right. Too many of you misinterpret 'minimalism' as 'soulless and empty'. Living rooms are so-named for a reason – they shouldn't feel cold and unwelcoming, but should be somewhere to stretch out and relax. And they need to feel 'lived in'. This doesn't mean household junk scattered throughout your home, but is about injecting some soul and creating a sense of comfort. This can be achieved physically through furniture and carpets but also visually through bright accessories, warm colours and soft fabrics. Your design needs to be both beautiful and practical, striking a balance between form and function.

DOCTOR'S ORDERS

- **Declutter – use clever storage options that double as furniture.**
- **Clean, clean and then clean again.**
- **Add ambience by incorporating plants, pot-pourri and scented candles.**
- **Rearrange furniture to maximize the space.**
- **Use mirrors to add light and emphasize key features.**
- **Define your space. If it's a dining area, buyers need to know.**
- **Ensure lighting is sufficient. Use brighter bulbs or change fittings if necessary.**
- **Use colourful accessories to make a room feel lived in.**

CASE NOTES: LOFTY AMBITIONS

The main living area in this loft-style apartment was a dramatic and versatile space but was not shown off to best effect. There was an overall sense of crowding and confinement. The bookshelf was filled to bursting point, and the owner, whose hobby was making theatre costumes, had piled stacks of fabrics behind the sofa, blocking the cupboards. None of this suited the contemporary, minimalist feel of the space, and neither did the old-fashioned style of the furnishings

before

after

and the random placement of furniture and objects around the room. This gave the decor a very bitty, disjointed appearance, particularly in such a large, open-plan space.

I began by making the owner divide her things into 'appropriate' and 'inappropriate' objects – those that could be used when the makeover was completed and those that could be stored. Buyers can find it difficult to envisage how they might use an open-plan space so we separated the area into different 'zones', dividing off a small office area from the living space with a wire mesh screen. To emphasize the living zone we repositioned the sofa and removed its old patterned cover to reveal a plain white fabric beneath. We covered the cushions in a vibrant red fabric to make red the room's new accent colour. Then we made some storage boxes, covered in the same red fabric as the cushions, which could double as extra seats. The white walls were given a fresh lick of antique cream emulsion, making the apartment a prime example of House Doctor principles: neutrals accentuated with stronger colours – in this case cream walls accented with red fabrics.

SEE ALSO

Colour	p36
Finishing touches	p66
Lighting	p106

B

BACHELOR PAD

For many people the term bachelor pad conjures up images of a chic, stylish headquarters for some swinging hipster on the prowl. In reality, the typical British bachelor pad ranges from the chrome-filled gadget warehouse to the dark, unloved pit. Either way, their owners are not going to have potential girlfriends *or* potential buyers. But all is not lost; with a good clean, a neutral colour scheme and the right accessories, it's possible to bring a woman's touch to even the manliest of bachelor pads. That doesn't necessarily mean robbing a bachelor of his identity – your widescreen TV is safe, boys, it just shouldn't be the room's focal point. Likewise, your precious CD collection isn't going anywhere, except perhaps into a modern tower unit. Buyers need to imagine themselves in your home, which means depersonalizing and giving the space a more neutral feel.

DOCTOR'S ORDERS

- **Dark leather and chrome don't work for everyone. Incorporate soft fabrics and neutral furniture.**
- **Keep wiring from TVs and stereos hidden away.**
- **Keep it clean. Scrub all traces of your party lifestyle from the property.**
- **Use modern, attractive storage options to house CDs and DVDs.**
- **Keep the colour scheme bright and neutral.**
- **Bring life into the rooms through plants and flowers.**
- **Replace dark bed linen with bright, fresh alternatives.**
- **Depersonalize.**

CASE NOTES: LAD'S PAD

The owner of this bachelor pad was a work hard, play hard type of guy, and domestic presentation was not at the top of his agenda. The hallway was dingy with a filthy carpet. The bedroom had furniture that was too big for the room and no bedside table. The small, functional kitchen had no eating area. The bathroom was one that you left feeling dirtier than when you went in. And the living room had a midden pile of magazines, bare walls, mismatched furniture and not a finishing touch in sight – plenty of crumbs but no comfort.

To improve the first impressions we replaced the hallway carpets and repainted the walls to make the space feel bigger and brighter. The master beroom was revamped with a new, neutral carpet, two bedside tables and slim-line wardrobes. As well as repainting the walls and units in the kitchen, we added two stools that sat neatly under the worktops. The bathroom was thoroughly cleaned before a new vinyl floor, shower screen and accessories were added to make it a place you wanted to linger in. The living room was transformed with very little effort or expense. We kept the existing furniture but steam-cleaned the sofa and dressed it with cushions that set off the accent colour in the room. Finally we added some new finishing touches that changed the room into the chic modern space that it was crying out to be.

before

SEE ALSO	
Clutter	p34
Depersonalize	p50
Neutralize	p121
Storage	p142

after

BATHROOMS

Bathrooms must appear as clean, light and spacious as possible. They must look up-to-date. The idea of having to undertake expensive modifications can put some buyers off. Improve the look of your suite by improving what's around it.

Get rid of strident colours or busy wallpaper by repainting. If the tiles are what's letting the room down, repaint them with a specialist tile primer and paint – a very simple but effective cure. Carpet soaks up water, with the result that it never looks its best and very often smells. There are lots of fabulous tiles that you could use instead, including sheets of beautiful mosaic.

Ensure the bath, basin and lavatory are clean. If any enamel is chipped, cover it up with specialist paint. Add a new shower curtain. Hide or throw out everything that's inessential here – all indispensable personal items should be stored out of sight. Attend to any minor jobs in the bathroom such as a dripping tap, a broken toilet seat or a loose towel rail.

Look at the treatment of the windows. Stick-on plastic etching can be an effective way of maintaining privacy while admitting light. Blinds should be kept clean and operational, and curtains unobtrusive. Make sure there's a light over the bathroom mirror and from the ceiling (operated from outside). Sometimes just replacing them with a more modern design can make a surprising difference.

Now you're ready to dress the room, neatly position a few well-chosen accessories. Fresh, fluffy towels are a luxurious must, as are new bars of soap. Pot-pourri and scented candles can help add a suggestion of other, more sensuous possibilities. If you replace your plant, make sure the new one is green and thriving. And last but not least, leave the loo seat firmly down – apart from anything else, in Feng Shui terms this will prevent you losing wealth.

10 BEST TIPS FOR BATHROOMS

1

No bathroom can be too clean, so use all your elbow grease to get surfaces really fresh and sparkling.

2

Declutter all surfaces. It's not necessary – or interesting – to have all your most intimate requirements on display.

3

Get rid of fitted carpets. They absorb moisture, often look tatty and smell bad.

4

Use only water-resistant floor coverings here – lino, marmoleum, vinyl, ceramic or mosaic tiles.

5

If the tiles round the bath and basin are showing their age, apply a coat of specialist tile paint to bring them up-to-the-minute.

7

Ensure your privacy in the bathroom with a new blind on the window, or install frosted glass or plastic film for that frosted effect.

10

Badly stained or soiled grout should be cleaned or, if it is in particularly bad condition, recoloured.

6

Pot-pourri, scented candles and pretty fragrant soaps and oils add something sensual to the atmosphere.

8

Finish off all DIY jobs and install additional lighting and storage, if necessary.

9

Purchase a new shower curtain, toilet seat and fresh, coordinating towels.

B

BATHROOM TRANSFORMATION

before

Putting a rug in front of a toilet is totally unhygienic; it just soaks up the dirt and smells.

Replace old towels, flannels and bathmats with a set of neatly folded, fluffy new ones.

A wicker basket makes an ideal container for rolled towels, and a wooden bucket is great for brushes.

DIAGNOSIS

Although it was not the worst example to feature on House Doctor, this bathroom certainly had scope for improvement. As is often the case, there was inadequate storage for towels and toilet requisites, with a spray can and a baby wipe dispenser on the floor. It had the potential to be a lovely light room but the natural daylight was leached away by a dark, space-shrinking green lino, partially covered with an unhygienic rug. The green-painted walls and yellow pine bath panelling and loo seat added to the general dinginess of the room.

TREATMENT

Taking my lead from the white tiles that covered half of the walls, I decided to swap the pine toilet seat and bath panel for white plastic ones, which helped to make the room feel more spacious. Out went the green lino in favour of a beige, mosaic-effect, vinyl floor-covering. The walls were painted a stone colour to tone with the flooring. Extra storage was provided in the form of an L-shaped shelf made of MDF and painted white. For towels and brushes I added a wicker basket and a wooden bucket, natural materials which toned with the walls and floor and helped to soften the whites in the room, preventing it from becoming too clinical.

after

Make your bathroom inviting by keeping it squeaky-clean. Every surface must be glistening.

BEDROOMS

Your bedroom is the most personal space in your house, and if you are selling it will have a strong influence on how buyers perceive your home.

Maximize the space so the room looks as large as possible. Present it in a way that will appeal to the greatest number of people. By day, it should be fresh, light and bright. Strident colours, patterns and floral prints on the walls are out – they make the room look smaller. Walls and carpets should be replaced with warm, neutral shades where necessary.

Look at the way the furniture is arranged. Minimize the number of pieces or the space will seem cramped. The bed should be positioned so that it doesn't block the door or the window. Clear the top of the wardrobe of all junk and consider if it would be better placed against another wall. Put away any clothes you've left lying around. If you share the room with your pets, find them a new sleeping space.

It's worth investing in new bedlinen, which will look great and reinforce the impression that this is a house you've loved and taken care of. If you don't want the added expense, at least make sure that what you have is clean and ironed.

Take your colour scheme from something in the room, such as a picture, and plan your accents from that. Add a few finishing touches – perhaps cushions at the head of the bed or a throw, neatly folded at the foot; scented candles, pot-pourri or fresh flowers will also add to the atmosphere.

If you're showing your room in the evening, make sure your lighting is effective. Directed right, it can help disguise the worst features by highlighting the best ones. Bedside lights are often more effective than a ceiling light. Check that all the lampshades are clean and the light bulbs are all working. Candles always give a flattering light and provide an enticing atmosphere.

10 BEST TIPS FOR BEDROOMS

1

Walls should be painted a warm, neutral colour, such as a soft peach, apricot or apple green. Strong colours and patterns may overwhelm a buyer and put them off.

2

Clear all clutter. But this is the one room where it is OK to display a few well-chosen personal photos.

3

Replace a worn carpet with a new one or, if the floorboards are in good condition, sand and stain them and invest in a couple of accent rugs.

4

Make a feature of a window with a view, framing it with a pair of attractive, colour-coordinated curtains.

5

Arrange the furniture so that the room appears at its most spacious and maximum light comes through the window.

6

Buy a set of new bedlinen or make sure the linen that you have is clean and well ironed – this will give the impression that you care for your home.

7

If you're transforming a former junk room into a second bedroom and require a bed, beg, borrow or even hire one until your sale is complete.

8

However much you love your pets, remove them from the room. You may not notice their smell, but it can be extremely off-putting to potential buyers.

9

Complete the whole transformation with the addition of pot-pourri, scented candles or essential oils ... but just one scent per room, please.

10

Check your lighting. Make sure the shades are clean, the bulbs work and that the lighting highlights the best features in the bedroom.

BEDROOM TRANSFORMATION

before

The pine furniture was out of scale with the room and just had to go – along with its associated clutter.

The bedding was a tangle both literally and metaphorically, with its mismatched patterns and styles.

The abstract provided a focal point above the bed and inspired the colour theme for the new bedding.

DIAGNOSIS

This master bedroom was part of a scruffy, neglected bachelor pad, and boy did it show! Unkempt, unplanned and unloved, it failed to work on all counts. Although it was a double room with a double bed, it gave out strong signals that it was nothing more than a single room, and so was unlikely to appeal to couples who came to view it.

The first thing that struck me on entering the room was how cramped it felt for a master bedroom. This was mainly caused by the oversized pine furniture squeezed into the space beside the bed and under the sloping roof. Neither the chest nor the wardrobe could be accessed easily, which explained the piles of clothes scattered around the room. There was no space for a bedside table, which is essential in a double room, and the curtains were hanging off their rails. The bedding was a mishmash of patterns and included an undersheet improvised from a duvet cover! Although the walls and floor were acceptably neutral, there was nothing to give the room character or definition.

TREATMENT

If it was to both look good and function well, this bedoom really needed turning round, beginning with the bed. We got rid of the pine furniture and reoriented the bed so the bedhead was under the alcove formed by the sloping roof. We painted the wall of the alcove a light brown to highlight this architectural feature and turn it into a selling point. Unusually shaped rooms such as this often call for imaginative storage solutions. We installed built-in slimline birch wardrobes that were easily accessible, and there was now also room for a bedside table.

To give the wall definition and to create a focal point, we put a large abstract painting above the bedhead. Its blues and beiges worked well with the furniture, and also provided the theme for the bedding - a contemporary beige, brown and blue duvet with co-ordinating cushions and a throw, and *two* matching pillows. Bye-bye bachelor crash-pad; hello stylish double bedroom.

SEE ALSO

| Display | p58 |
| Finishing touches | p66 |

after

CHILDREN'S ROOMS

Bringing up children can be a chaotic experience and all too often this is reflected in their rooms. Potential buyers won't share your toddler's love of cartoon wallpaper and rainbow furniture. There's no need to disguise the fact that it's a child's room, but buyers need to see the potential. Incorporate sturdy, versatile furniture which will stand the test of time, restrict bright colours to items like pillow cases and accessories, and offer hints to alternative uses for the room. Incorporate space for a child to play but make sure there's enough storage to pack the toys away before a buyer comes calling. If the room is cluttered with items your child never uses or has grown out of, donate them to charity – there are plenty of children who could make good use of them. Keep the room tidy and simple – preparing a house for sale isn't rocket science, it's child's play.

DOCTOR'S ORDERS

- Keep décor simple – avoid childish patterns.
- Incorporate sturdy, long-lasting furniture.
- Choose easily cleaned, washable fabrics.
- Build in plenty of storage.
- Add colour through curtains, bedding and accent items which can be easily replaced later.
- Useful, adaptable furniture can double as storage.
- Hint towards alternative uses for the room – a computer, for example, suggests a potential office.
- Put unused toys in storage or donate them to charity.

before

CASE NOTES: A MILITARY OPERATION

This bedroom was nothing less than hideous. The camouflage décor totally dominated the room and was decidedly off-putting. The bed was leaning against the wall in pieces, giving the impression that this wasn't even a child's bedroom, but more of a messy storage space or play area. Once we had emptied the bedroom, I could work out where to begin if a buyer was to see the potential of the room.

The first, most obvious job was to paint over those camouflage walls. I decided on a seaside theme, so the walls were painted blue and I used accessories such as a lifebelt and some bright plastic buckets on one shelf and tiny coloured beach huts on another. The owner finally assembled the bed and placed it next to the wall. A jaunty, red-striped duvet cover chimed with the carpet and curtains, both of which were already in the room but barely noticeable under the chaos.

As a nod to the family's army connections, I allowed an orderly row of toy soldiers back onto one of the shelves, but now they looked a little upgraded given their new surroundings. I decided to take the computer from the living room and give it pride of place in a corner. The room now clearly gave the message that it could be used as a small second bedroom or even as an office.

C

CLEANING

When selling a house you need to appeal to a buyer's senses – everything should look clean and smell fresh. That means putting some effort into it and scrubbing every surface. Buyers don't want a second-hand bathroom, so concentrate on making yours look brand new. If you have carpet in the bathroom, get rid of it – new lino is inexpensive, easy to fit and a whole lot more hygienic. The kitchen is just as important. Buyers need to feel they could move in and prepare a meal there, so every inch should be clean enough to eat dinner off. And give your carpets a new lease of life by hiring a carpet steamer.

DOCTOR'S ORDERS

- **Wooden flooring can be cleaned with one part methylated spirits, one part vinegar.**
- **Remove candle wax by placing paper towels over the wax and ironing.**
- **Ink stains can be neutralized with nail polish remover.**
- **Soak up any red wine spillages, then clean the area immediately with white wine.**
- **Remove chewing gum by freezing it. Pick off the frozen gum then dab the area with methylated spirits.**
- **Water and vinegar applied with an old piece of newspaper is perfect for cleaning windows.**

MAKE IT SPOTLESS

Elbow grease can add more value to your property than almost anything else. I can't over-emphasize how important it is to clean, clean and then clean some more when you're selling your house. The kitchen and the bathroom are the two most important rooms to get absolutely spotless, but it shouldn't stop there. Dust every surface, ornament and lampshade that you possess. Make sure that the ashes are removed from the fireplace and that a fire is newly laid. The fire surround, whether tiles, slate or marble, should also be grime-free.

LEFT Scrub the sink, the bath and the toilet bowl, and don't forget to clean the area immediately behind the toilet seat. Wipe the splashbacks clean and ensure that any mirrors in the bathroom are left sparkling.

BELOW By putting some effort into cleaning you are making your home a much more pleasant place to be in (for you as well as any potential buyers), and also prolonging the life of your household items.

C

CLUTTER

Clutter is one of the curses of modern living, and will do you no favours if you are selling your home. Each room's clutter is different in nature. The living room and dining room will usually be cluttered with books, ornaments and CDs. In the bedroom the biggest offender is the wardrobe. Not only could you probably dump half your clothes, but the wardrobe can also be filled with old luggage and mementoes. The kitchen might have cluttered work surfaces and cupboards full of old food and redundant appliances. Children's rooms are a storehouse for outgrown toys, books and clothes. And lastly, the bathroom – here the biggest offenders are unused cosmetics and cleaning products, as well as tatty linens.

CASE NOTES: LAUNDRY DINER

This lean-to conservatory provided a much-needed additional space, but was clogged with clutter and woefully underused. Its primary function was as a laundry room, but it was also home to the vacuum cleaner, clothes airer, child's scooter and pets' feeding bowls. Truth was, it had become a dumping ground, a sort of giant cupboard, for anything that couldn't be stored within the house, on the assumption that 'out of sight is out of mind'. But there is no excuse for any room, including a utility area, to look like a pigsty. If you are selling your home your viewers will look at such spaces even if you choose to ignore them.

The other problem with the room was that it was a real waste of space. Utility rooms are often small, with little scope for anything else, but this one had the potential to be a real living space. Large, light and with good views, it would make a superb conservatory-dining room, without sacrificing its utlity role. The first job was to hide the washing area, which we did by partly boxing it in and adding curtains across the front. These hid the equipment while allowing easy access when needed. A white-painted wooden top and shelves provided surfaces for plants, ornaments and storage baskets for the cleaning paraphernalia. We painted the other woodwork white to create a cleaner, more modern feel, and added fabric blinds to the ceiling. These softened the light and disguised the plastic roof. All we had to do then was install a dining table and chairs, and presto! – a cluttered dumping ground was transformed into a classy dining area, with a secret laundry when required.

before

after

COLOUR

Colour is of primary importance in every design; it can alter a room's mood and affect its sense of space and light. To make a room look bigger, avoid heavily patterned wallpapers or carpet; they make a room feel claustrophobic. Stick to light colours with minimal patterns to add the illusion of space. Painting low ceilings white should help make the room feel taller. Brighter colours can be added in moderation to a neutral room on accent walls and through artwork, soft furnishings and accessories. Take time when choosing fabrics for a room. Neutral colours that you see together in the natural world will always complement each other. Blocks of colour will bring a room to life, and a simple change of tone, texture and pattern can completely change the feel of a room.

COLOUR MOODS

Warm colours such as reds, yellows and oranges are cosy but can make rooms appear smaller. Cooler colours like blues, greens and whites make a room seem larger but can also feel unwelcoming.

Reds warmth and passion
Oranges reassurance and warmth
Greens nature, calming freshness
Blues cool, calming, soothing
Yellows sunshine, energy
Browns natural, solid, practical
White clean, airy, spacious
Greys smart, urban, contemporary

USING COLOUR

Cool colours, lighter values, and plain or minimal patterning make walls and ceilings recede and create a spacious feel. Dark or bright colours, or loudly patterned wallpapers or carpet, make a room seem smaller. A few tricks will enhance the sense of space. If the ceilings are low, paint them almost white (add a touch of yellow, as ceilings tend to grey out in their own shadow) to visually raise them, or use vertically striped wallpaper. Avoid horizontal borders. If ceilings are too high, add a dado

rail or painted wallpaper border to the wall two feet below the ceiling. Paint the ceiling and up to the border the same medium to deep tone.

A disproportionately long room can be made to look shorter by painting the two end walls a deeper or warmer colour. Generally, the most spacious-seeming rooms incorporate little pattern, have pale walls and carpet and, to prevent the room from looking too impersonal, use colour in accessories as accents.

ABOVE Pale blue walls, white woodwork and turquoise accents in the cushion and fireplace create a cool, sophisticated look.

LEFT Accent colours can be added to a room in several different ways.

COLOUR SCHEMES

Colour is a very personal thing. Everybody brings their own associations to different shades, which is exactly why if you are thinking of decorating before selling, you shouldn't impose your taste on any potential buyer. A bright blue might remind you of your Australian holiday, but others may find it cold and uncheering. If you have a strong colour scheme in a room, try to tone the wall colour down so that it harmonizes and becomes less obtrusive. This generally tends to make the room look bigger, too.

DOCTOR'S ORDERS

- **Oil-based gloss – hard-wearing, shiny finish for woodwork, indoors and out.**
- **Oil-based eggshell – matt finish for interior woodwork.**
- **Acrylic gloss and eggshell are water-based variants. Quick to dry, but not as durable as oil-based paints.**
- **Primers and undercoats – use on any bare wood before applying top coats.**
- **Water-based emulsion – for interior walls and ceilings.**
- **Solid emulsion – easy to apply. Non-drip, so good for ceilings, but costs more than regular emulsion.**
- **Specialist paints – if painting radiators, tiles or floors, make sure you get the appropriate paint.**

MIX AND MATCH

Try a new colour out in at least three areas of the room so you can see how it looks in changing lights. Remember that paint usually dries one or two shades darker than when it is first applied. However, if you're looking at a room with a total personality by-pass, it's not too late to establish a colour scheme by introducing coloured accessories. A confident combination of cushions and/or throws,

LEFT The colour wheel is an
extremely useful tool when it
comes to choosing paints. If you
choose colours from the same side
of the spectrum ('related colours'),
they will blend naturally together,
creating a soothing and
harmonious atmosphere.
However, if you want to create a
more vibrant effect, pick colours
that are opposite each other
('complementary colours'), being
careful to use different strengths
of tone so they complement one
another rather than cancel each
other out. Though the colour
wheel illustrates how colours
work alongside each other, it's
all a case of personal choice and
it can be fun experimenting with
less orthodox combinations.

OPPOSITE The neutral décor of this
bedroom is livened up by adding
pink curtains and scatter cushions
in a matching colour.

rugs and carefully picked ornaments can introduce harmony and
character. And a neutrally decorated room is perfect if you are the sort
of person who likes to change the colour scheme of a room regularly –
rather than altering the colour of the walls you can simply change the
colour of your accessories to introduce a new feel to a room.

If you're unsure about which colour to use with another, consult
the colour wheel (see above). Although you may favour energizing
bright colours from opposite sides, in this instance it would be wiser to
use harmonizing adjacent shades to create a calm and relaxing mood
in the main rooms. Don't make the mistake of slapping on a coat of
white paint as an easy solution. Though it might be seen as a safe
background colour – or non-colour, as it contains no colours at all –
it can look bare and uncompromising and will subtly alter in shade,
depending on the contents of the room and the light. Much better
to go for soft neutrals and pastels that will blend with what's there,
keeping the atmosphere without intruding on it.

COLOUR SCHEMES

before

CASE NOTES: KITCHEN COLOURS

This sickly pink kitchen was enough to turn a buyer's stomach and I can't say I'm surprised. The owner claimed she was known as 'the dizzy blonde who lives in the pink house', and she'd certainly let her personality run riot in here. This heavily stencilled cerise nightmare needed toning down and I chose a fresh green which gave the room a light, natural feel and was much better suited to a kitchen. The new colour transforms the room, perfectly complementing the light wood of the existing units. Appropriate artwork and coordinated accessories help finish the job and the result is a buyer's dream.

SEE ALSO

| Colour | p36 |
| Kitchens | p98 |

RIGHT With the addition of the breakfast bar, the kitchen had been transformed into a kitchen-diner and the pinboard reflected how it was now viewed as more of a social space.

FAR RIGHT As a finishing touch, place mats and glasses that tied in with the new green colour scheme were added to the breakfast bar.

after

COLOUR SCHEMES

CASE NOTES: TONING IT DOWN

This bedroom was known jokingly by the owners as the 'tart's boudoir', but in terms of getting the house sold this was no laughing matter. Bright pink walls decorated with dragonfly stencils, bedding that bordered on the magenta, shocking pink drapes, a golden cherub, a garish red carpet – it was all too personal and too much, and it clashed horribly with the pine furniture. This decor might have been intended to be 'romantic' but it wasn't going to woo potential buyers.

The key task here was to tone things down with a more restrained colour scheme. We had to give any possible buyers the chance to imagine *themselves* inhabiting the room. To this end we painted the walls in a warm, subtle shade of peach and laid a new, neutral carpet, both of which were more sympathetic to the pine. The bedding was allowed to stay but it was curtains for the drapes, stencils, cherubs and other items littering the room. Accenting touches of pink and red were allowed back in the form of cushions, throws and the owner's theatrical costumes.

The cushions on the bed were a mishmash of colours and shapes, providing an object lesson in how not to use finishing touches.

before

Once we had successfully toned down the decor we added decorative objects and spots of the owner's favourite colours to give the room personaltity and interest.

after

LEFT With a neutral backdrop and the removal of the fussy drape, the elegant iron bedhead became more of a feature.

CURTAINS AND BLINDS

Curtains have many uses – they frame and enhance a window and its view, they help keep the warmth in a room, they act as a shield between you and the world outside and they control the amount of light that enters. Blinds give a clean, uncluttered look on their own but can also work well with curtains to provide privacy or shade. They are particularly useful where curtains are hard to fit, for instance in dormer windows.

MEASURING UP

Measuring up correctly is vital. To find the correct width, do the following:

1 **Measure the length of the track, including the overlapping arm if there is one.**
2 **Decide how full the curtains will be by choosing a heading (see facing page).**
3 **Multiply the required width by the fullness to get the overall fabric width required.**
4 **Divide this by the width of the fabric you have chosen to reach the total number of widths required.**
5 **Measure the length of fabric drop, allowing extra for pattern repeats and hem.**
6 **Multiply the fabric drop by the number of widths to reach the total length of fabric needed.**

CHOOSING CURTAINS

The style of curtain you choose should relate to the style of your room. Take into account the period of your property, the design of your furniture and the existing décor of the room. Take your time in choosing the fabric. Make sure to take sample swatches home so you can test them in the light of the room and against your colour scheme. The ideal curtain length is either to the floor or to the windowsill. Anything in-between will not flatter the proportions of the window. You can play with the dimensions of the window by your choice of curtain. A narrow window will look wider if the curtain rail is extended on either side and sill-length curtains are used, while a wide window can be narrowed with floor-length curtains and/or those that cover part of the glass when open.

Curtains should run to the bottom of the windowsill or, for a more elegant look, to the floor.

ABOVE Thin muslin curtains provide privacy, but don't obstruct the light flow.

LEFT A tieback can be made of metal, of the same fabric as the curtains, from a contrasting fabric, or it could be a richly tasselled rope.

CURTAIN ACCESSORIES

Headings, pelmets and poles should be combined to maximum effect.

HEADINGS

Headings are the gathers at the top of the curtain. The most simple is a gathered heading about 2.5cm (1in) deep. Pencil pleats (about 7.5cm/3in deep running across the curtain) and pinch pleats (small groups of pleats at regular intervals) are the most popular. For a more formal effect, you can use box pleats, goblet pleats or lattice pleats. Other types include: looped/tab-top headings (loops/tabs that circle the pole); cased headings (two parallel rows of stitching across the top hem create a slot for a curtain pole); wooden, plastic or metal rings sewn directly onto the fabric; or simple fabric ties.

PELMETS

Pelmets cover the curtain headings or tracks and can be as simple or as fancy as the mood takes. They are usually made of wood and can be cut into shapes that complement the window. Covered with fabric or just painted, they can help make a more formal statement.

TRACKS AND POLES

Take as much time to choose your curtain poles or tracks as the curtains themselves. Poles can be plain or decorative and come in a huge range of materials and diameters. Make sure the track or pole is strong enough to bear the weight of your chosen fabric.

FABRIC

Never skimp on fabric to save money. Generous curtains look best, so choose cheaper fabric rather than less of it. Large patterns suit big windows and heavy fabrics work best full-length. If you're stuck, try plain cream curtains edged with coordinating fabric.

TIEBACKS

These are useful to hold the curtains back out of the way. Whether you want a simple metallic or wooden holdback or a more elaborate fabric tie will depend on the style of your curtains.

CURTAINS AND BLINDS

CHOOSING BLINDS

Roller blinds are the simplest type of blind and have the advantage of going with most decorative schemes. You can buy them in easy-to-make kit form. Make sure you choose a tightly woven fabric that will unroll evenly. Alternatively, you can treat a softer material with fabric stiffener. On larger windows, check that the fabric you choose is substantial enough to make the blind hang well. Remember, too, that roller blinds are not usually very successful on a long drop, for instance on a French window.

The choice of fabric can make a big difference to the effect created. For a clean and businesslike look in an office or study, select something plain and smart. For a warmer, homelier look, choose patterns. Plain blinds, especially, look more 'finished' with the addition of an edging. This can be a fringed, braided or scalloped edge, or simply a band of contrasting colour.

ABOVE Roller blinds are practical, easy to fit and come in every colour imaginable.

RIGHT Even a simple Roman blind such as this one can add visual interest to a space.

TYPES OF BLINDS

Blinds are a sleek way to dress windows. Available in many colours and materials, they are especially useful where space is limited.

ROMAN BLINDS

Roman blinds are an unfussy solution as versatile as the roller blind. When pulled down, Roman blinds look like their cousins but they pull up in deep folds. Because of this, the 'look' is a bit softer, and many people prefer Roman blinds to the simpler roller blind in living spaces or bedrooms. Unlike roller blinds, Romans are usually lined to make them hang better, with battens sewn into pockets at regular intervals up the back.

AUSTRIAN BLINDS

Austrian blinds are the most ornate. They are unlined, often have a scalloped hem and pull up in swags, sometimes with frills at the side or bottom. They may be left at half-mast, and 'soften' a room. This makes them a perfect choice for bedrooms or any room that you want to be cosy. Because they cover quite a lot of window, they are a clever way of disguising an ugly one.

VENETIAN BLINDS

Now available in a wide variety of different styles and colours, Venetian blinds don't have to look dull and functional. The ones with narrow slats are immediately much smarter, and thin-slatted metallic blinds can look wonderful with a hi-tech design – a new kitchen, for example – or can give an up-to-the-minute look to a study. And they provide a lovely effect when the sun shines through.

WOODEN SLATS

The 'Earth Mother' alternative to Venetian blinds, wooden slats are usually held by bands of webbing or canvas which come in various colours and textures. Each of these will have a different effect in your room. They go well with stripped floors, natural wood furniture and ethnic fabrics. They are also practical and, when closed, keep in warmth. Louvred shutters are beautiful and serve the same purpose.

White Venetian blinds let in light and provide privacy without interfering with the lines of a room.

Louvred shutters are at the more expensive end of the scale but are undoubtedly elegant.

DECORATION

A common mistake when decorating is to concentrate on individual elements and lose sight of the overall design. Decoration is more than a new coat of paint – it covers everything from painting and wallpapering to furniture and floor treatments and beyond. Each element needs to complement the other to create a consistent, coordinated design. For example, if you've made a bold statement through your choice of wallpaper, it makes sense to redecorate other elements in a warm but neutral colour. If you can't afford to replace furniture then your new colour scheme needs to complement what you already have. Alternatively, consider recovering or repainting existing furniture. Choose a starting point for your design from something in the room, perhaps a favourite ornament or piece of artwork, and plan your accents from that.

DOCTOR'S ORDERS

- Choose paint colours carefully, taking into account a room's existing furniture and furnishings.
- Choose a starting colour and coordinate accents from there.
- Don't trust colour charts – paint a piece of MDF and move it around the room to view it in different lights .
- Complete all odd jobs before painting.
- Consider staining dark furniture a lighter shade.
- A well-chosen rug can visually harmonize décor.
- Always try to keep the bigger picture in mind.

CASE NOTES: LESS IS MORE

This master bedroom was a cacophany of colour and pattern. The purple colour scheme of the bedding, drapes and curtains was far too overpowering for the size of the room. And there was just too much going on visually, with a jazzily patterned runner behind the bed, a duvet with a different pattern, and a cast iron-iron bed that was a striking piece but introduced yet more lines and patterns. All these disparate elements combined to create an unbearable sense of visual clutter, with nowhere for the eye to settle even momentarily. This bedroom was about as restful as a motorway intersection.

The problems with the décor in this room could be solved with some simple arithmetic. We needed to subtract the garish colours and confusing patterns and add more restful tones and more considered finishing touches. A new, relaxing colour theme of aqua and beige was inspired by a piece of wallpaper, which we also framed to create some art for the walls. The theme was carried through by repainting the walls, changing the bedding and replacing the curtains. The eye-boggling runner behind the bed was sent packing, and some brown scatter cushions and a beige rug were added to tie the scheme together. Thus transformed, this was now a stylish, inviting, and most importantly a relaxing bedroom.

before

after

DEPERSONALIZE

When selling a property you have to remember your home is no longer your own. Buyers want to imagine themselves in your space and that means you have to take your personality out of it. Your children might be the most important thing in your world, but family photos and children's drawings are just a distraction to buyers. Hide them away. Likewise your personal collection of porcelain poodles, china teapots or whatever other crazy thing you Brits like to collect. Buyers are looking for a neutral, depersonalized space they can make their own.

before

ABOVE The leopardskin print and quirky lighting reflected the owner's personal tastes too strongly and had to be removed.

SEE ALSO

▶▶ Neutralize   p121

CASE NOTES: NOTHING PERSONAL

This room was set in a stunning period property, where a buyer had every reason to expect grandeur. Despite this I felt the living room lacked a necessary sense of comfort. The way that the furniture was arranged made the space seem smaller than it was. The blood-red walls and the furnishings at the window area were too strong and personal. They drew the eye away from everything else in the room. The roller blinds hardly did justice to such a wonderful bay either.

In general, this house wasn't on the critical list, but because the price was high, buyers would be picky so I needed to pay attention to

after

the detail. The window was an important feature in the room, but I felt it was underexploited. Bright red obviously appealed to the owner, but it could easily have been offputting to a number of buyers who might not want to embark on a repainting job. A harmonious palette is generally more appealing. So I toned the area down with a light green which blended in with the rest of the room. The windows themselves were imposing enough to deserve special treatment. This time we went to the expense of ordering custom-made blinds, which transformed the bay into a more elegant and inviting spot.

I went on a search-and-discover mission in the rest of the house, finding beautiful pieces of furniture that suited this room better. By moving the existing furniture around, removing some and thinning the contents of the shelves right out, the room immediately felt larger. The decorated cabinet and mirror made a delightful vignette against a difficult wall, the mirror helping to create the illusion of space.

STORE IT!

Whether it's a mountain of soft toys, an avalanche of antiques or a priceless hoard of Beatles memorabilia, your personal treasure trove won't help sell your house. Carefully pack everything away and store it in the attic or shed or in a commercial storage facility. A few choice items may set off a room but the rest will have to remain hidden until you've sold your house.

D

DINING ROOMS

The dining room is often one of the most under-utilized rooms in the house. It may double as anything from a home office to a children's playroom or even a temporary bedroom. But that's not what potential buyers want to see. By smartening it up and defining its function, you will give people an opportunity to imagine what life might be like if they buy your house.

Declutter and clean the room thoroughly first. You must make it look inviting, warm and sophisticated. Its purpose should be immediately obvious. If the walls are overpowering or shabby, repaint them in a safely neutral colour. A bright green carpet won't be to everyone's taste. Replace it with something more neutral or, if the floorboards are sound, sand and varnish the surface. Keep the furniture in the room to a minimum so that it's possible to walk around or sit at the table with ease. If your table has doubled as a desk or a work surface, you might cover it with a smart tablecloth or runner.

Look at your dining room chairs. If you can, get them to match and ensure the seat covers are not showing the remains of previous parties. Making new seat covers for loose seats is an inexpensive and simple job. Simple cushions are another way to give an impression of comfort. The fabric should tie in with the colours of the curtains or even repeat it. It's a good idea to lay the table but make sure you use your best matching china, glasses, cutlery and napkins. Anything less will look untidy and uninviting. Go for a simple vase of flowers instead.

If your house lacks a dining room, try and define a space for one. This may mean giving up a small area in the kitchen, living room or even the hall. To underline your message, lay the table simply but elegantly so it's clear where eating can be enjoyed. If you pay attention to these important details, you will add to the intrinsic value of your home.

D

10 BEST TIPS FOR DINING ROOMS

1

If you're fortunate enough to have a separate dining room, don't let it double as an office, play room or box room while your home is being marketed.

2

Freshen up old dining chairs with smart new seat covers or even add small, comfortable cushions.

3

Don't crowd the room with furniture. It should be easy to walk round the table.

4

If you need to freshen up the walls, choose colours that are warm and invite dining and entertaining. If using wallpaper, make sure that it's not too busy or overpowering.

5

Cover a particularly tatty table with a new tablecloth or table runner.

6

Avoid clutter, especially on the table and tops of furniture, so that people will find it easy to imagine themselves sitting down to enjoy a meal there.

7

If there is no separate dining room, find a space that could be used as a dining area and define it with table and chairs.

8

If you don't have a table and chairs, beg, borrow or hire them – this is an essential part of selling a lifestyle.

9

Fresh flowers in a beautiful vase placed in the centre of the table will give it focus.

10

Lay the table with coordinating napkins and china to issue a subliminal invitation to your viewer, but try to keep it simple.

DINING ROOM TRANSFORMATION

DIAGNOSIS

This imposing dining room hardly invited buyers to sit down and enjoy a meal. It was dark, dingy and overflowing with books, knick-knacks and various holiday souvenirs that the owners had collected over many years. The dresser was totally cluttered, packed with the owners' personal collection of china – which was probably rarely used – as well as a fruit bowl, a lamp and other unnecessary items.

This, combined with the busy mantelpiece and a bookcase that was full to the brim with books, photos and other personal effects, made the whole wall of the dining room nothing more than a large and chaotic storage space. Underneath, though, I suspected there was a light, spacious dining area waiting to get out and impress the buyers.

The clutter on the dresser swamped a good-looking piece of furniture.

Space was created for the piano by moving the dresser away.

A few well-chosen items of china replaced the previous chaos.

before

after

TREATMENT

Firstly, I needed the owners to make some tough decisions. I asked them to remove their collection of china and put back just a few of the best pieces, and boy did it make a difference. The newly spacious dresser was moved to the other wall, freeing up the alcove for the piano. The mantelpiece was then cleared of vases and pictures and replaced with a couple of classy candles. The mirror was removed, which made extra space for one of the owners' own paintings to be placed above the fireplace.

Next we uncovered the original parquet flooring and cleaned it with one part methylated spirits and one part vinegar. It was then waxed. The wallpaper was painted cream and the net curtains removed to let in more natural light. That just left the dark bookcase, which we replaced with a small table and a couple of pictures.

DISPLAY

Displaying collections such as china, silver, tins or ornaments needs to be thought through carefully. Having too many pieces crammed into a space does neither the space nor the objects justice. All it shows is the impressive size of the collection and the fact that you don't have room to accommodate it. If necessary, rotate the collection so that it can be truly appreciated. A large collection can be displayed in different rooms.

ABOVE Give your books room to breathe and the whole bookcase will become a design feature in itself.

OPPOSITE Contemporary shelves such as this allow you to mix and match books with other well-chosen items.

BOOKS

Books furnish a room but not if they are stuffed randomly into shelves or left higgledy-piggledy on tables or the floor. They can bring colour, texture and definition to a room if they are given proper space.

When planning to house your books, think of the shelving as a design feature and not just as a necessity. The inside of a bookcase might be painted a different colour to that of the walls, or wood might be stained to match the furniture in the room. Objects displayed beside your books will offset their shape and create a sense of depth and space in the room.

Bookshelves are useful for bringing elements in a room together or framing them. They can frame doors or windows, and if they are built into alcoves on either side of a chimneybreast, bed or window seat, they will frame a focal point. Shelves can also act as focal points in themselves, for example cubed shelves arranged in a geometric pattern against a wall become a feature.

If you are buying furniture, think about how it might be used for books; a small bookcase, for example, can double as an occasional table by a sofa. A sofa in the middle of a room might back onto a low bookcase rather than a table. The space beneath a window seat or bed could be converted into bookshelves. A wide passage between rooms or a stairway might be transformed by the addition of floor-to-ceiling bookcases. Remember, this sort of library needs to be well lit so that it doesn't seem poky and so that the contents of the library can be seen. Wherever you place the shelves, do not overcrowd them. Take time to weed out the books you're unlikely to read again and give them to charity.

PICTURES

If hung well, pictures lend character and warmth to a room. Single pictures may be hung symmetrically, possibly balancing a mirror or a piece of furniture. If you don't want a regimented sense of order then create a more asymmetrical look by visually balancing a large picture against a number of smaller ones, remembering that each side of the composition should take up the same square footage.

When using pictures to create an impact, bear in mind that a strong unifying look can be achieved by using the same frames and mounts. If they are unevenly sized, the composition needs to be worked out before hanging the pictures on the wall. Measure the wall space you want them to occupy, then lay the pictures on the floor to occupy the same area, working out the right balance. If unsure, make paper silhouettes and tape them to the wall first to see the effect.

SHELVING

If you have only a few books, or wish to display other items such as photographs or ornaments, shelving is a practical solution. There are numerous types available, ranging from a full track system that takes up a whole wall to simple wooden shelves secured by brackets. Shelving can be tailored to fit in with the character of a room or positioned so that it is a main feature. Ensure that the materials and fixings you use are strong enough to take the intended load.

DIVISION

When you're dealing with a space that's used for more than one function – a dining room-cum-living room, for example, or a large kitchen-diner – it pays to separate particular areas and give them a sense of individual purpose. Look for natural divisions in the room like large alcoves or partial walls, or create your own divisions using furniture, such as bookcases or box shelving. Folding screens are also effective, especially the translucent ones, which create a sense of division without blocking out the light or breaking up the space too much.

DOCTOR'S ORDERS

- **Define areas using colour – subtle differences in shade can create a visual division.**
- **Use lighting. A suspended ceiling light over a dining table, for example, can be used to distinguish a dining area from a living area.**
- **Use the shape of a room to define areas.**
- **Shelves, bookcases or dressers can be used to break up a room.**
- **Screens add division whilst retaining natural light.**
- **Rugs are useful for defining zones within a space.**

CASE NOTES: SCREENED OFF

This was a spacious, airy room but there was too much going on in it. Different styles and objects were vying with one another for attention. The formal table and chairs and the cosy suite rubbed up uneasily against the oriental treasures brought back from the owners' travels. There were too many things detracting from the feeling of space, making it hard to appreciate fully either the room or its wonderful contents. The elegant fireplace was almost completely hidden behind a small statue. And even though the flat was too high up to invite the stares of neighbours or passers-by, it really needed curtains or blinds.

We went through the owners' belongings, weeding them out, rehanging pictures and arranging a few key pieces so each one could be highlighted and individually enjoyed. Despite the undoubted quality of their foreign treasures, there was no need to have them all on display. I restored the fireplace as the focal point of the room by removing the statue that was blocking it.

It was such a large space that I felt we could afford to distinguish the living and dining areas. I find screens are often very effective because they give a feeling of division without being obtrusive or obstructing the light. In this case, I wanted to give the room a bit of pizzazz so I designed a screen based on the nearby Brighton Pavilion. The frame was made from MDF and painted to look like wood by dry-brushing thinned brown paint over a yellow base. The panels were then filled with a hemmed fabric.

before

after

DOORS

A door can be a strong focal point for a property, both externally and internally. It is the architectural feature that introduces you to the space behind it and provides the first clue to what you might find in there. Make a feature of your front door – painting it doesn't cost much and can lift the appearance of the exterior of your house. If it is painted the same colour as the windows, it will lose impact. Much better to choose a strong colour, matching the frame with the window frames. Bear in mind the colour of your neighbours' doors, too – clashing colours can look awful.

DOCTOR'S ORDERS

- Check that the style of your doors suits the period of your house.
- All door fittings and furniture – hinges, handle, knocker, etc. – should match and be polished thoroughly.
- Replace any fittings that do not work.
- Decorate interior doors, with for example contrasting panels and beading or stencilling on the frame or panels.
- Don't block doors with furniture or clutter.
- If a door isn't essential, remove it and make an archway; eradicate all signs of the hinges, which are easy to forget.

DECORATIVE OPTIONS

Apart from dividing one room from another and maintaining privacy between those spaces, doors can also be decorative. They can break up the monotony of a wall. Would your door look better if the frame or the panels were a different colour? Alternatively, if the walls are busy, you might want the door to blend into the background by painting it the same colour as the wall or extending bookshelves to run over the top of it. Don't block doors with pieces of furniture. It's important that the flow of the home is efficient, making any newcomer feel more comfortable there. Ask yourself if all the doors are absolutely essential. An archway may be as effective. Consider a tie-back curtain on an iron rod – it can be both elegant and space-saving. Or you might replace door panels with glazing. You'd be surprised how a dingy hallway can be made lighter and much less claustrophobic, even if you use etched, smoked or coloured glass.

LEFT A small window in a front door can make a significant difference to a dark hallway.

ABOVE A sheer curtain covering a doorway into a dark hallway can both lighten the hall and keep the kitchen area separate.

ABOVE LEFT Door fittings that match gleam in welcome on this traditional panelled front door.

FAR LEFT If a door is constantly left open, it may make sense to remove it altogether and create a feature of the resulting archway.

LEFT Ensure your doors match the style and period of your home, and give them a new lease of life with a fresh coat of paint.

E

ESTATE AGENTS

Once your property has been spruced up and is ready to sell, you are not out of the woods yet – it's time to find an estate agent. The right agent can make the difference between your home selling quickly at the right price or languishing on the market forever. While the agent must be a good salesperson, he or she also needs a basic grounding in finance, law, building and, occasionally, even interior design – and should have the relevant experts at his or her fingertips when necessary.

ABOVE A good estate agent will know the area well and will be able to give you a realistic price based upon what similar properties have sold for recently.

HOW TO CHOOSE AN AGENT

There are so many estate agents operating, it's hard to know which one to pick. So to find one you can trust and rely on, it's worth spending a little time doing your research first.

Choose a specialist It's important to select an agent who specializes in your area if your property is to be valued at its correct price and given high local visibility. Also, the agent needs to be knowledgeable enough to answer any questions a potential buyer may have about the surrounding area.

Keep in touch Let the agent know you're serious about making a quick sale.

Avoid using friends or family However good an agent a friend may be, if something goes wrong your relationship may not stand the strain. It is far preferable if someone you know can recommend an agent based on experience.

Choose someone you can trust Look for an agent who meets your particular needs as they will be representing you to the buying public. Selling a property is an emotional event. You need to feel your agent is someone to whom you can always relate.

Be selective Take time to interview at least three agencies. Ask them exactly how they are going to market your home and, of course, how they would value it. And don't forget to ask about their charges.

Do your research Ask if you can contact previous clients for references, and request a list detailing the sales the agent has achieved in the past 18 months.

Protect yourself Only employ an agent who is a member of the National Association of Estate Agents in order to protect yourself if a problem arises later on.

Don't skimp Remember that you usually get what you pay for. Don't automatically choose the agent charging the lowest commission.

Hedge your bets For greater exposure, you may want to use more than one agent, but always remember that quantity probably won't produce quality of service.

Expect the best Make it clear from the outset exactly what you expect of your agent. This way, you run little danger of being let down.

Work together Finally, having chosen your agent, cooperate as best you can and try to avoid any misunderstandings. After all, you're both working towards one goal: the swift and successful sale of your home.

DIY SELLING

More and more people are cutting out the middle man and selling their homes over the Internet. Websites offering 'one-off' costs to advertise your property are common, and many provide a 'virtual tour' of your home online. Saving on estate agents' fees may appeal, but make sure you research the area thoroughly and always read the small print. Another way of saving money is to do your own conveyancing; however, it is a long, drawn-out process and your mortgage lender will want a guarantee that everything is in legal order. One option is to do the groundwork yourself and call in a professional for the final stages.

FINISHING TOUCHES

Once you've achieved that all-important neutral background, largely by eliminating bold colours and patterns or too many contrasting colours on the walls of a room, it's time to look at the accessories you can use to build colour back in. Accessories can carry a colour theme through your house, pulling the look of each room together. You must ruthlessly remove all the expendable bits and pieces and only replace with things that are essential to the look. Check in the back of your cupboards. I've seen forgotten wedding gifts come into their own at this moment.

ADDING ACCESSORIES

If you are really stuck, it's time for a bit of retail therapy. Go easy, though – if you're planning on selling you don't want to confuse your buyer into thinking they've walked into a bazaar. Cushions, throws and ornaments may brighten up a living room in moderation, while fluffy towels, new soaps and a shower curtain can transform a bathroom. You may want to colour-coordinate a few items on the kitchen worktop – kettle, toaster and storage jars, for example. New candles look good in almost every room and can be used to introduce colour. Candlesticks can reflect the style of the house, traditional or modern. Use large pictures or a mirror on a blank wall. Accessories make the difference between a bland, uninteresting house and a vital, desirable home.

LEFT The look of a room can be pulled together by coordinating the curtains and cushions, or throws and cushions.

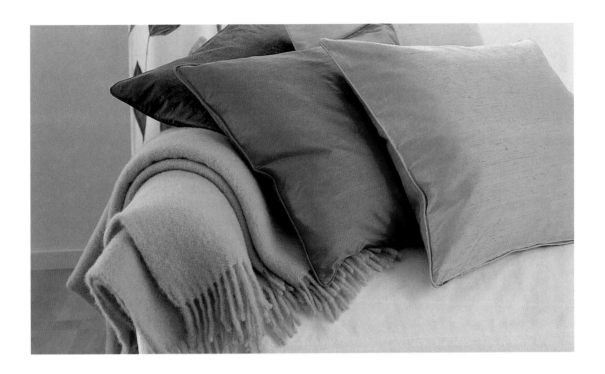

ABOVE Colourful cushions and throws make the perfect finishing touch and can transform the appearance of a room.

LEFT Don't underestimate the effect of fluffy new towels and bathmats – they add colour and a welcome touch of luxury. Check that you've thrown away all those old bits of soap and replace them with some beautifully scented new bars.

F

FIREPLACES

A fireplace can definitely add value to your home. As well as being a practical heating source, it always provides an interesting focal point to a room. Any existing fireplace should be properly cleaned and you should make sure that it's not being blocked from view by furniture. If the fireplace surround doesn't fit the period of the house or style of a room, visit an architectural salvage yard where you may be able to pick up something suitable at a reasonable price.

DOCTOR'S ORDERS

- **Use the finest grade wet and dry paper to take surface discolouration off a marble surround. Wet the paper and use very carefully.**
- **A decent brand of instant coffee mixed with a little water will work to stain a wood surround or match paler patches.**
- **Rake out the grouting between tiles and regrout before washing the tiles with soapy water.**
- **Black grout is good for fireplace tiles as it won't be stained by smoke. Alternatively, stain the existing grout black.**
- **Repolish all cast-iron work with graphite paste.**

A simple wooden fire surround, varnished or painted as desired, is an inexpensive way of making a fireplace into a feature.

A blazing fire never fails to give heart to a home, creating warmth and a cosy atmosphere.

FIRESIDE OPTIONS

If a fireplace has been boxed in, it's often worthwhile restoring it to its former glory. The same goes for that empty hole left when one has been removed. You could complete the look by investing in a fireguard and fire dogs. Light the fire if it's appropriate. Remove all the invitations and general junk from the mantelpiece where there is room for a well-chosen ornament or two – at most! Complete the look by hanging a large mirror or painting above.

SOURCES

MARBLE HILL FIREPLACES
70-72 Richmond Road
Twickenham
Middlesex
TW1 3BE
Tel: 020 8892 1488
Fax: 020 8891 6591
www.marblehill.co.uk

ELGIN & HALL LTD
Adelphi House
Hunton
Bedale
North Yorkshire
DL8 1LY
Tel: 01677 450100
Fax: 01677 450713
www.elgin.co.uk

**COX'S ARCHITECTURAL
  SALVAGE YARD**
10 Fosseway Business Park
Moreton in Marsh
Gloucestershire
GL56 9NQ
Tel: 01608 652505
Fax: 01608 652881
www.coxsarchitectural.co.uk

WEBSITES
www.edwardianfires.com
www.fireplaces.co.uk
www.victorianfireplace.co.uk

ABOVE The Mexican tiles around
this dining room fireplace stood
out when the clutter in the rest of
the room was edited down.

LEFT A fireplace with a mantelpiece
to display favourite ornaments is
the perfect centrepiece to a room.

F

FIRST IMPRESSIONS

A well-maintained and decorated exterior provides a wonderful welcome to you and your visitors and shows the pride you take in your home. It is particularly important if you want to impress a potential buyer. Most buyers make up their minds within the first 30 seconds of entering your home, so first impressions are all-important. Your interior might be perfect but if you have an unkempt garden, scruffy exterior paintwork and filthy front windows, a buyer may not even bother knocking on the door. Luckily, all these things can be easily fixed. Mow the lawn, tidy the edges and invest in some attractive bedding plants. Repaint or Revarnish the front door and polish the letterbox, knocker and door handle. Make sure windows are spotless and window sills clear of clutter, and check curtains and blinds are evenly drawn and properly hung.

DOCTOR'S ORDERS

- **Remove that rusty old car or caravan from your driveway and store it somewhere else.**
- **Make sure the boundaries between you and your neighbours' properties are clearly defined.**
- **Throw out and replace any dead plants.**
- **Clear away any sign of pets.**
- **Prune any trees that have overhanging branches.**
- **Mend broken guttering or clipped roof slates.**
- **Make sure all windows are spotless.**
- **Invest in a nice new 'Welcome' mat.**

CASE NOTES: SIMPLY A MESS

The whole façade of this house was in urgent need of major first aid. The building work had been left incomplete, the front door was dull and uninviting and the filthy old curtains at the front window and lack of curtains elsewhere made the house look unloved. The paintwork was in terrible condition, both on the frames and the stonework. The car parking area was unfinished and made the path to the front door muddy and unattractive. We cleared away the rubble and painted the windows and front door, which made the house look fresh and inviting. Then we hung new curtains, built a low wall to separate the parking area from the path and added a climber on a trellis.

RIGHT The ugly piles of rubble heaped up outside the bay window indicated that the owners cared very little about first impressions.

before

ABOVE By constructing a low brick wall – made from stock that matched the house – there was now definition between the parking area and the front path.

after

SEE ALSO

▶▶ Appearance   p14

F

FLOORING

Because flooring is a semi-permanent fixture in a home, you should spend some time thinking about various factors before choosing a style. Will it fit in with the period of your house? Is it going to get heavy use? Do you want to lay different surfaces in each room? There's a huge range of carpets and other materials to choose from, so before you decide, think about what the rooms will be used for. If you're planning on selling, the choice and condition of your floor coverings say a lot about you to the buyer.

DOCTOR'S ORDERS

- **Replace kitchen and bathroom carpet with something hard-wearing and easy to clean, such as tiles (vinyl or ceramic), lino or wood.**
- **Choose neutral colours so that the carpet fades into the background.**
- **Remember what the room is being used for when you choose the floor covering.**
- **You will need a hard-wearing carpet for the hall and stairway.**
- **A dark staircase and hall can often be dramatically improved by a lighter, neutral shade of carpet.**
- **Stain and varnish floorboards or paint them with specialist, hard-wearing paint.**

MYRIAD CHOICES

If you're putting your house on the market, you won't be living with your floor covering forever, so don't go for the bright red or sunshine yellow that you love. Choose the plain, the neutral, the understated. These are unlikely to offend a buyer's eye and have the advantage of apparently enlarging the floor space too. Seagrass matting can be a practical alternative, if a little unfriendly to bare feet and crawling babies. Should the idea of investing in some carpet be too daunting, look at the floorboards beneath. Bare varnished boards often look great with a couple of rugs thrown on them. Rugs are also a good way of bringing together the colour scheme in a room. In the kitchen or bathroom, the floors should clean up thoroughly or you should replace the covering. Whatever you use should be waterproof and hard-wearing. Again, there's a huge range of choice, but err on the side of the neutrals. The flooring should always recede into the background, letting your furnishings speak for themselves.

Your carpet can play a big role in a successful house sale. A carpet that is dark or heavily patterned dominates a room and makes it seem smaller. A smelly, damp carpet in a bathroom is a real turn-off. Dining rooms with food trodden into the floor are out, as are carpets that are old and worn. A new carpet may seem an unnecessary expense, but it will lift the appearance of the room and your buyers won't be imagining the extra cost of replacing it themselves. Make it easy for them to like your house.

Coir matting comes in different weaves, which provide interest in an otherwise neutral floor covering. It is hard-wearing, sound absorbent and ideal for any room except the kitchen and bathroom.

A combination of Amtico and hardwood offers a floor treatment with a difference.

A floating hardwood floor looks classy and provides a clean and modern finish for all rooms.

With a vast range of contemporary designs available, linoleum has come a long way since the 1950s.

Amtico floor tiles offer an excellent, hard-wearing, easy-to-clean finish. Plus they're easy to replace.

SOURCES

AMMONITE FLOORING
22 Hayes Street
Hayes
Kent
BR2 7LD
Tel: 020 8462 4671

AMTICO CO LTD
Kingfield Road
Coventry
CV6 5AA
Tel: 0800 667766
www.amtico.co.uk

CERAMIC PRINTS LTD
(floor tiles)
George Street
Brighouse
West Yorkshire
HD6 1PU
Tel: 01484 712522

CRUCIAL TRADING
PO Box 10469
Birmingham
B46 1WB
Tel: 01562 743747
www.crucial-trading.com

WEBSITES
www.alliedcarpets.com
www.carpet-online.co.uk
www.naturalcarpetsltd.co.uk
www.ukcarpetsdirect.com

FLOORING

The light-coloured floor and white units provide a good backdrop for luminous spots of colour.

CASE NOTES: LIGHTENING UP

This living area was part of an open-plan lounge, dining room and kitchen. Not a large space to begin with, it was made to feel claustrophobic because of the inadequate storage, mainly dark furniture, lavender walls and rusty-red carpet. The ceiling, which was quite low to begin with, had been artexted with a busy pattern, and the combined effect of the floor, walls and ceiling was to make it seem as if the room was closing in on you. With an open-plan room, it's important to create a light and open space, but this was anything but.

This sense of claustrophobia was repeated throughout the house, and it was obviously turning off potential buyers. When we visited, it had been on the market for six months and the owner had not received a single offer, and this despite three price reductions. When people notice this happening in the property ads or the estate agent window, they begin to think there must be something seriously wrong with a house, beyond the state of the decor.

DOCTOR'S ORDERS

- Unless you're buying a special water-resistant type, only fit carpet in areas where it will not come into contact with liquids.
- Think about the style of your home and its colour scheme before choosing a particular carpet.
- A neutral carpet can be livened up by the addition of a colourful rug.
- Ensure that you choose a tough carpet for your stairs.
- Save thick-pile carpet for the bedrooms, where it will get less wear and tear.
- Consider carpet tiles; they are relatively inexpensive and easy to replace.

before

after

It was clear that a lightening-up exercise was needed, to show what
an appealing place this could be, particularly the lounge. Here we
repainted the walls in a shade of mushroom and softened the pattern
on the artex ceiling. Then we replaced the rusty carpet with a beige
one, which brightened the room considerably. A smallish room like
this needs a unified storage system so we got rid of the free-standing
shelving and created a false wall with built-in shelves and recessed light
cabinets made from the existing dispay cases. This provided a focus for
the room and an integrated space for home entertainment equipment.

The sofa was stripped of both its OTT fake leopardskin throw and
its red cover, and then re-covered with smart new green and white
fabrics. The transformation was completed with new, coordinated
curtains and a roller blind.

F

FOCAL POINTS

Every room needs a focal point. It is the element that grounds the space and focuses your attention on entering. It gives the room a centre, and brings disparate elements together. Display a focal point well, arranging furniture and artefacts around it. It is possible to have more than one focal point in a room as long as one is subordinate. Focal points can also change with the seasons. A fireplace may be highlighted in the winter, while a plant or picture window could be the focus in the summer.

FIREPLACES

If your room has a beautiful fireplace, make the most of it. Remove any clutter that may be obscuring it, clean it thoroughly and polish any fire irons or surround. Focus attention on it by clearing the mantelpiece of accumulated photographs, invitations and general detritus, and arranging only one or two objects in their place. Hang a large mirror or picture above it so that the eye is not distracted by too many different elements. A fire always gives the subliminal message that the living room is the heart of the home, but if you are unable to light one, burning candles in the grate can be equally attractive. Arrange the furniture around it, so that it becomes the unmistakable centrepiece of the room.

FEATURE WINDOWS

Another focal point might be a stunning view through a window. Emphasize it by dressing the window appropriately. It might be enough simply to paint the window frame a contrasting colour. Otherwise there are all sorts of blinds, curtains and drapes that could be used. When dressing the window take into account its size and the style of the rest of the room. Swags and tails will not look good in a minimalist environment or on a modest casement window. Other ways of drawing attention to the window might include the addition of a built-in bay window seat, window boxes on the outside ledge, a single table in front of the window or an ornament on the ledge. Again, it is important to orientate the furniture so that the view isn't blocked by anything too large and the window can be seen from all vantage points in the room.

ABOVE Furniture such as this shelving unit can be a focal point, but ensure that the surfaces are uncluttered.

ABOVE RIGHT Hanging a picture or mirror above a fireplace will emphasize its importance as a feature.

Always leave plenty of room around a piece of artwork so that it does not clash with other items.

FURNITURE

If your room is not blessed with either a fireplace or a view worth highlighting, look at the largest pieces of furniture in the room. A dining-room table, an armoire, a dresser or a bed could all be the focal point of a room. The key is to ensure that the piece is positioned correctly. If the room is symmetrical, the focal point should be placed centrally. Tables should be beautifully laid or have a central decoration or runner. Beds need to be dressed with clean linen and scatter cushions that accentuate the colour scheme in the room, while cupboard doors should be firmly shut with nothing hanging from them. Dressers must display only a select number of objects.

WORKS OF ART

Sometimes a focal point can be created using one or more striking works of art. The focal point might take the form of a single painting or photograph, a carefully arranged group of artworks, or a sculpture. Painting one wall a different colour to the others will help to place the focus on artwork. Spot-lighting can play an important part in enhancing a sculptural work. A neutral decorative scheme is best for showing off a work of art. Too many clashing colours and patterns will compete with it and prevent it from being the star of the show.

F

FURNITURE

If you are selling your home and your rooms look a bit empty, buy, borrow or rent furniture until you move – new furniture will look better and can go with you to your new home. Move furniture around until the area looks spacious and uncrowded. Pieces from other rooms may help. If a sofa dominates the room, it may be worth replacing it with a smaller model to give a greater feeling of spaciousness. Tired old sofas and armchairs that look as if they've lost their bounce can be brought back to life simply and inexpensively with smart throws, slipcovers, or the addition of coloured cushions. Cushions come in limitless sizes and shapes and are useful for introducing colour, texture and comfort. They can coordinate or contrast with the other surfaces and colours in a room.

DOCTOR'S ORDERS

- Avoid oversized, marshmallow sofas that eat up the space in living rooms.
- Dark, dated furniture never looks good, but is especially bad in bedrooms.
- If you have a dining room, fill it with a dining table rather than leaving an empty space.
- Instead of buying new items, simply rearrange a room – it can make all the difference.
- Similarly, move furniture around the house to harmonize style and colour.
- Re-covering furniture in appropriate fabrics can also bring new life to tired furniture.

FORM AND FUNCTION

The furniture you choose should suit the function of each room. A living room, for example, is geared mainly towards relaxation and may need nothing more than a comfortable sofa and armchairs. However, you might want to consider whether the room will be also be used for entertaining, a likely scenario if you don't have a dedicated dining room. If this is the case, and you have the space, you might want to include a dining table and chairs, though if you're only going to throw the occasional dinner party then you can probably get by with a folding table and some stackable chairs.

Coffee tables come in many different styles and, as well as being a useful platform for cups and magazines, they can also be a practical storage space if you invest in one with a shelf. You might prefer a nest of tables instead, locating it in the corner of a room and bringing one out when it is needed. Take the height of tables into consideration if you have young children who might bash into them; you may wish to opt for rounded rather than sharp corners to reduce the risk of injuries.

You may also need something to hold your television/dvd/video player. This could take the form of a basic stand, though there is an increasing trend towards all-encompassing units which completely enclose the audio-visual components inside. And as an advocate of not making a TV the focal point of a room, I highly recommend them!

The kitchen is often the busiest room in a house, so you should do some careful planning to ensure that it is not crowded with furniture. If you're lucky enough to have a large space, the main feature will be a table and chairs, but you may instead have a simple, yet practical breakfast bar. Ensure that the areas around the work surfaces, fridges and ovens are clear of furniture so as not to disrupt the flow of those preparing food.

A dedicated space for eating is becoming less common in modern households, but dining rooms will, by their very nature, include a table and chairs, possibly more formal than those found in a kitchen. They may also have a cabinet or dresser in the room in which to store cutlery and to place dishes on before or after a meal.

Bedroom furniture should be well thought-through to provide the most comfortable sleeping/relaxing space possible. Aside from a bed, wardrobes, drawers and side cabinets are the main elements. If there is space for a table and chairs, this can be incorporated into a teenager's bedroom so that the room doubles up as a study area.

ABOVE A formal dining area requires space around the table and very little other furniture.

BELOW Living rooms are versatile spaces, so should include furniture that reflects the different activities that take place within them.

F

FURNITURE

CASE NOTES: MAKING THE UPGRADE

This Victorian terraced house had a lot going for it, combining original period cornicing and fireplaces with contemporary features such as stripped pine floors and an open-plan living/dining room. However, it was let down by its decor and more particularly by the furniture. The living room was a case in point. The peach walls were a bit too intense and the bulky leather three-piece suite dominated the room.

I felt this needed to be a more sophisticated and soothing living space so we repainted the walls in a light sage colour, which complemented the wooden floor. The bulky furniture was replaced with new, elegant pieces, including a wing-back armchair, which better suited the style of the house. The sofa was more modern, but its rolled arms and light colour echoed the style of the armchair. Furniture needn't match exactly as long as the shapes, colours and textures complement each other.

ABOVE The bulky leather furniture was inappropriate for the style of the house, which demanded something more sophisticated.

before

LEFT The wing-back armchair, upholstered in a white fabric, combined elegance with modernity. A simple birch side table worked well with the armchair and sofa, and with the clean, light décor.

GARDENS

Whether used as an outside space for entertaining, a play area for children or simply a plot to cultivate plants and flowers, a garden can provide you with hours of enjoyment. But to keep it looking good requires a certain amount of effort. This is especially true if you intend to sell your property. If it's looking a bit shabby and you want a quick sale, it's time to address the problems. Buyers must be made to want to come into your house and not drive straight past it.

Tidy up the garden (front and back), removing all signs of children, pets and rubbish. If necessary, define the boundaries of the house with the addition of fencing. Prune trees if you can. They look better and will let more light into the house. Make sure the windows are clean and curtains are straight.

No matter how small your garden may be, you must make the most of it. Quite simply, it represents cash in your pocket. Providing an extra outdoor room will add value to your house. Now's the time to clear the overgrown garden – tidy up existing plants, brighten things up with some border plants and cut the lawn. If necessary, lay some new turf.

Invest in some garden furniture and make an area where it will be pleasant to sit out and entertain. If you live in the city and have access to a roof terrace, it is just as important to turn it into a haven away from the chaos of urban life. Make sure the area is kept clean and tidy. You need pot plants (bought or hired) to create the right atmosphere. A small outdoor table and chairs are essential.

Always remember that when in the garden, your potential buyer will notice the back of the house, so carry out the same checks as you did for the front. Painting the back door is a good idea, and a nice finishing touch is to position a potted plant beside it to make it look cheerful and welcoming.

10 BEST TIPS FOR GARDENS

1

Define your boundaries. Buyers need to know exactly what they are getting for their money, so if necessary, invest in some new fencing.

2

Mow the grass, weed the flowerbeds and purchase some flowering border plants to give life and colour to the dingiest garden.

3

Make sure you have adequate lighting, both at the front and at the back of your home.

4

Don't forget about how your house looks when viewed from the garden - paint exterior walls a bright, welcoming colour.

1

2

4

5

Turf over your children's football pitch and keep them off it until the house is sold.

6

Make an area where you can put a garden table and chairs. This will immediately transform a garden or conservatory into another area that can be enjoyed in the sun.

7

Paint your front and back doors and polish all the door furniture so it gleams. It immediately suggests that you take as much care inside your home. And be sure that your house numbers are easily visible.

8

Put a container or two of flowers, or a hanging basket, as a welcome by the front and back door.

9

Consider adding an interesting water feature, an attractive garden light or even some garden sculpture as a finishing touch.

10

Have a regular weekly maintenance programme to keep the outside of your home looking great throughout the whole marketing period.

G

GARDEN TRANSFORMATIONS

before

The makeshift plant stand meant the plant balanced precariously.

The makeover resulted in an area that was ideal for socializing.

DIAGNOSIS

This small urban garden was a pleasant enough space but it was a little tatty and was not being used very efficiently. The plants were in various states of health and had been arranged along the edges, with some placed haphazardly on garden tables. As a consequence, the garden lacked a focal point. In addition, the paving looked green and potentially slippery and some of the slabs were starting to raise up rather dangerously. All in all, the space needed a general tidy-up and some life injecting into it.

TREATMENT

We started by transforming the surface of the patio area. The flagstones were taken up and replaced with white gravel, which produced a fresher, more informal look. This inexpensive treatment immediately brought a sense of life into the garden. The flowerpots were edited down, with only the healthiest of plants surviving the cull, and some new plants and contemporary planters were introduced into the space. The dead area along one side of the fencing was converted into a sheltered arbour where large, squashy cushions begged to be sat on. A focus was created by placing a café-style table and chairs in the middle of the space, which tied in well with the feel of this town garden. As a final flourish, a soothing water feature was added.

after

G

GARDEN TRANSFORMATIONS

DIAGNOSIS

More a plant cemetery than a roof garden, this outdoor space needed urgent treatment. Space like this is at a premium in a busy city and it's madness not to make the most of it. Having gone to all the trouble of having the terrace designed, the owner had completely lost heart during a spell of bad weather and failed to finish it off. A cracked marble table, a few miserable straggling plants and a naked gazebo did not make an earthly paradise.

Contemporary garden ornaments can make a stunning impact.

Make a bold and colourful statement with a brightly painted fence and lush hanging baskets.

before

Even in winter, flowering plants can be bought to cheer up a neglected outdoor space.

after

TREATMENT

This was the only outdoor space belonging to the house so it was important to make the most of it. Although it was winter when we went to work, the first port of call was the garden centre, where we chose a number of plants, some for colour and some for presence. I particularly liked the bamboos, which are delicate, whisper in the wind and grow quickly. The pots were already on the terrace so it was just a question of filling them with the most appropriate plants until it began to look more like a garden space.

I had plans to use the table inside the house. However, the cracked top lent easily against the terrace wall to disguise some pipes. Instead, we brought up a round table, which I felt went better with the space, its curves echoing those of the gazebo and providing a contrast with the angular shapes of the terrace itself.

Otherwise, all that was required here was a good sweep to make the place look loved and cared for and a slight rearrangement of the furniture and statuary. It's attending to such small details as these that can add hundreds of pounds to the sale of your house.

The green of the foliage worked well against the white walls and the wood of the decking.

HALLS AND ENTRANCES

If your hall is used as a dumping ground for every inanimate object that crosses the threshold, now's the time to clear it. For those thinking about selling, tripping over bicycles, shoes, umbrellas and schoolbags won't endear your house to any potential buyer. Never underestimate the importance of properly presenting your hallway – it is the valuable space that sets the tone of your home and it's vital to make a good first impression.

Your hall should appear as light and welcoming as possible. Paint the walls a fresh, neutral colour that leads effortlessly into the rooms beyond. My favourite trick for enlarging a small hallway is to hang a mirror, which adds to the impression of light and space. Also, make sure the lighting is as effective as possible. Check all the bulbs have decent shades. A windowless hall will benefit from a halogen light, which gives maximum brightness. If you do have a window, place a single plant on the sill rather than a few that block out the light.

A hall carpet wears down quickly. If yours is particularly shabby, replace it – to economize, you could use an offcut or perhaps look at the possibility of sanding and varnishing your floorboards instead, and using new carpet only on the stairs. If you can't get rid of ugly features, disguise them instead. A radiator looks far better when it's boxed in and the ledge is a useful place for storing letters.

Don't crowd your walls with pictures; they will make the walls seem to close in. Hanging one or two carefully will do the trick and provides a welcoming touch. And don't forget the stairway. Ensure that warm, neutral walls and good lighting issue an invitation upstairs. Check that the carpet is securely fixed and that any handrail is firmly secured to the wall.

10 BEST TIPS FOR HALLS AND ENTRANCES

1

Remove all clutter so the passage into the house isn't restricted and the door opens freely.

2

Repaint dark, claustrophobic halls with a warm, paler colour to maximize the existing space and light.

3

If the floor covering shows signs of wear, get rid of it. Can you use the floorboards or tiles underneath? If not, recarpet the area.

4

A fresh green plant or vase of flowers strategically placed at your front door adds a bit of life as well as a welcoming touch.

5

Don't crowd the walls with pictures. It'll make them close in. A couple of well-chosen ones are usually enough.

6

Be sure that the lighting (both natural and artificial) is sufficiently bright, but not glaring. Update if necessary.

7

The stairs should lead invitingly upstairs, so consider whether it's worth investing in a new stair carpet. Replace missing banisters and, if necessary, smarten them all up with a lick of paint.

8

Create a focal point by boxing in a radiator and using the shelf for a couple of favourite ornaments. This will break up the longest hallway.

9

Open up narrow hallway spaces by maximizing both artificial and natural light, and ensuring nothing blocks the route.

10

If you have a burglar alarm, box it in or relocate it, so that it's not the first thing visitors notice upon entering the house.

HALLS AND ENTRANCES TRANSFORMATION

before

Clear up any clutter, such as bags, papers, bottles, prams or toys, that bars the way into the house.

Boxing in the radiator turned it into a more elegant feature and provided a shelf for letters and a trailing ivy.

DIAGNOSIS

This hallway did not say 'welcome', either to the owners or to possible buyers who came to view the house. And because first impressions are so important, that was not going to help with a sale.

Like many hallways this one was a dumping ground for bags, coats and anything else that happened to be dropped off there. Door handles and hooks have very different roles in life, which in my opinion should never be confused. The internal doors were 1970s office-style – a look that may make a comeback some day, but not in my lifetime. The green walls did nothing to bring light into what was a dingy, narrow space. And I've never seen a worse place to put a bookcase – right by the front door, so that anyone who came into the house immediately felt hemmed in.

TREATMENT

The first chore was to remove all the clutter. A hall should draw you or your buyer into the house without having to sidestep bags and shimmy around shelves. Then we painted the walls in a creamy yellow, which would catch the sunlight when it streamed through the glass panels in the front door and make the hall brighter and more welcoming. We liked the idea of the decorative wallpaper border halfway up the wall, but added one with a less fussy pattern that toned with the walls. The office doors were painted white to coordinate with the front door and other paintwork and, again, to make the most of the available light. We boxed in the radiator to improve the general appearance of the hall, and thereby created a shelf for a trailing ivy (please note that a plant can only be used on such a shelf during the summer, when the heating is off). As a final touch, we hung a mirror above the radiator, which increased the light and the feeling of space.

As well as increasing the light and expanding the space, a hall mirror is useful for checking your appearance before going out.

after

INSPIRATION

Inspiration for your design and decorating scheme can come from almost anywhere. Look around you and consider which kinds of styles evoke positive reactions in you. Don't restrict your view to your home; I've known clients find design inspiration in modern hotels, country cottages and even a Chinese restaurant. Equally, a single piece of furniture or focal point in the home could be a perfect starting point. The trick is to establish what styles and colours inspire you and then incorporate them into a design you can live with. Magazines, books and brochures are perfect hunting grounds for inspiration, and it's well worth collating relevant images on a mood board.

MOOD BOARD

Creating a mood board is not only easy but it's also fun. Simply collect examples of the designs that turn you on. These could be cuttings from magazines, squares of fabric, paint swatches and even key words. Buy yourself a cheap pinboard and attach your images to create a picture of which designs, colours and styles interest you. Look for recurring themes and try to develop a unified idea of your own individual taste.

With a wonderful view through the window, it's easy to see where the owners of this property found the inspiration for the sofa cover.

JUNK

Junk has no place in your home; it belongs in a skip or on a tip. Whilst the rivers of clutter flowing through your houses may contain items you actually need and use, the chances are there's plenty of junk being swept along in the tide. The good news is there's no need to incorporate clever storage devices to accommodate it, no reason to build extra shelving – if you don't use it, lose it. If you can't give it away then throw it away. You'll feel lighter, refreshed and ready to tackle that more useful clutter.

before

CASE NOTES: TAINTED SPACE

Here a secondary bedroom was being used as the master bedroom, but I couldn't think of anywhere more unrelaxing to be. The place was full of junk and horribly untidy. I wanted to restore this bedroom to its rightful position as a secondary bedroom. By clearing away all the excess clutter and restoring the ironing board to its rightful place downstairs, the room could be seen for the decent size it was. We painted the walls, boxed-in the radiator and added some new soft furnishings to create a space that simply oozed comfort and relaxation.

after

KITCHENS

Whether doing up your home for yourself or presenting it for a potential buyer, there are certain simple things you can do that will make your kitchen look modern, clean and inviting. Think surfaces. Clear all but the most essential equipment from your worktops so there's plenty of space for preparing food. If you've used the tops of the wall units for storage, clear everything off.

The cheapest way to give a fresh new look to dark or dated wooden units is to paint them white. Gloss or soft sheen emulsion provides a practical, wipeable surface. Sometimes simply changing the handles is enough. If any of the doors or drawers have come adrift, fix them back. If you don't look after something as simple as that, who knows what attention you pay to the rest of the house?

If the walls have seen better days, repaint them, taking your cue from the tiles, curtains or flooring. Brightly coloured walls won't appeal to every buyer and take attention away from the room itself. If the floor has taken a beating over the years, replace it with a stylish and easy-to-clean covering. If showing the room at night, make sure the work surfaces are lit properly.

Then it's time to obey my first rule of thumb: clean, clean and clean again. Your kitchen MUST shine. Any curtains or blinds need to be taken down and washed or cleaned. Remove all signs of animal life. Many buyers will find the idea of animals in the kitchen unhygienic and off-putting.

Once the room is decluttered and spotless, bring in the colour accents. Coordinate a few key accessories: new dish towels, a bowl of apples (they last longer than most other fruit), toaster and kettle. If you've the space, showcase one or two things to create a stylish and welcoming room. And once you've transformed the kitchen into a room that anybody would want as the heart of their home, it's time to move on.

10 BEST TIPS FOR KITCHENS

1

Clean everything thoroughly. It's essential that your kitchen looks as hygienic and functional as possible.

2

Get rid of any evidence of where your pets eat or sleep. Some buyers might find it unhygienic or even positively offensive.

3

Finish off any minor repairs you may have started. It's important not to give the impression that an inexpensive new kitchen might need to be refitted in the near future.

4

Only have new, neatly folded drying-up cloths out on display – NOT the ones you've been drying your hands on all week!

5

Clear away all inessential clutter, including last night's washing up, and any household items that have gathered dust on the tops of the units.

1

5

6

If the units look dated, consider painting them or even replacing the doors or handles altogether.

7

Check the floor. It should be spotless. If it is worn, consider replacing it.

8

Make sure the room is as light and bright as possible. That means neutral-coloured walls with accents of colour in the room.

9

If taps, cooker or hob have seen better days, replacing them is not that expensive and can give a new look to an old kitchen.

10

Baking bread, boiling a cinnamon stick on the cooker or brewing fresh coffee adds an aroma that appeals subliminally to the buyer's senses. It creates that feeling of 'home'.

KITCHEN TRANSFORMATIONS

before

How impractical? These pots and pans were like a stack of cards.

Butchers' hooks are a versatile method of hanging implements.

DIAGNOSIS

This was one of the smallest kitchens I'd ever been in. Although there were some existing shelves and utensil hooks, they smacked too much of student DIY and were too solid to be doing the room any favours in terms of space. The work surfaces were crowded, which made a tiny space seem even tinier, and the focal point of the room was the washing up. Scrappy old towels hung on the radiator (beware, they can smell, too), upturned mugs and glasses festered on the draining board and the ugliest thing of all, a washing-up liquid container sat on the window sill. The kitchen looked cluttered and was a long way away from being an appealing place to prepare food.

Practical slatted shelves took up the dead space on one wall.

TREATMENT

Working on a budget, we couldn't refit a new kitchen to make better use of the space, so the only alternative was to make the most of what we had. Streamlining a small space can be surprisingly effective so, as with many other kitchens, the first thing to attend to was the general untidiness. The washing up was cleared away, as were the objects on the window sill; in their place came an attractive fern. The items on the work surfaces were also cleared and the well-used formica top was reinvigorated with some specialist paint.

The old shelving units were taken down and replaced with more practical units which were less intrusive. The strong colour scheme was replaced with white, which as well as lightening up the space provided a striking contrast with the blue shelves. Replacing the existing flooring with blue tiles completed the look.

after

KITCHEN TRANSFORMATIONS

DIAGNOSIS

This kitchen reminded me of bedsit days. It had a serious personality by-pass, not helped by a dull colour scheme, tatty paintwork and shabby old kitchen units. Even though the view outside wasn't great, the window was devoid of any sort of curtains or blinds, which only served to enhance the scruffy feel of the space. Even though I always recommend clearing clutter away, very occasionally it helps to leave some around – an empty kitchen looks unused and unloved. And boy, did this kitchen need some tlc.

Simply fixing new handles on units can make a big difference.

Glass storage jars are not only practical, but add an element of colour to a kitchen.

before

A contemporary kitchen unit can add the wow factor to a space.

after

TREATMENT

To start with, a light, contemporary paint treatment injected some life back into the space – it began to look as though it could be enjoyed again. A thin fabric blind was put up, which not only took the edge off what was behind it, but added a softness to the room while not depriving it of any light. Galvanized metal sheeting transformed the whole look of this kitchen. Easily attached to the unit doors, it immediately made them stylishly modern. A small but fashionable Shaker-style cupboard filled the dead wall space, its mesh door allowing a sense of space to be retained there. And finally, storage jars, utensils and flowers were added to complete the homely feel.

LIGHTING

Light and shade will be crucial components in the design of your home. Used cleverly they can highlight and disguise good and bad features. Lighting is often overlooked in the planning of a room, but remember it can change the atmosphere at the flick of a switch. The right lighting can bring a room alive or calm it down. It can be dramatic, soothing, romantic or just plain functional. It is up to you to set the tone.

ABOVE Uplighters cast soft light onto the wall of a room to give an ambient feel.

ABOVE RIGHT A large window will let plenty of light into a room, so coordinate your colour scheme with this in mind.

NATURAL LIGHTING

Watch the direction of sunlight entering each room and see how its effect changes throughout the day. Your choice of colours and arrangement of furniture should take this into account. Kitchens and living rooms benefit from having as much light as possible encouraged into the room. Clean the windows. Pull back curtains so they don't obstruct the light flow. Use light colours on the walls and furniture. In darker rooms, use gloss on the woodwork and hang mirrors to reflect more natural light into the space.

ARTIFICIAL LIGHTING

When planning the lighting in a room, you must think about the layout of the room, how it is used, the furniture present and the kinds of light that will suit the style of the room. Remember to take safety into account. You don't want accidents arising from badly lit kitchens or bathrooms, or from people tripping over stray flexes.

AMBIENT LIGHTING

Every room needs ambient or background lighting. Steer clear of central pendant lights because they can cast a rather bleak, unfriendly atmosphere. Ceiling downlighters or spotlights can be angled for the right effect and, if on a dimmer, can produce a practical bright light by day and a more soothing, intimate mood by night. If they are wired in separate circuits, you can dim one area of a room but illuminate another, governing the focus of the evening. For example, you may want to forget about the kitchen and concentrate on the dining table; then, after the meal, shift attention towards the sitting area without having to be reminded of the washing up. A different mood can be established by introducing subtle shadows. Table lights, standard lamps and wall lights can all be used to this effect. Wall lights or uplighters will wash the walls in a softer, more flattering glow.

TASK LIGHTING

You will need concentrated areas of light on work surfaces, desks and reading or sewing chairs. There are all sorts of spotlights on the market ideal for task lighting. You may prefer a desk lamp or a standard spotlight to light wherever you are working. Kitchen worktops can be lit by angled downlighters, halogen spotlights on tracks or fluorescent lights under the upper wall cabinets. Bathroom mirrors will need good lighting, too. And don't forget the bedroom – almost everyone needs a good bedside light.

An anglepoise or spotlight can be directed to highlight – or deflect attention away from – a particular area in a room.

DRAMATIC LIGHTING

You may also want lights to accentuate specific features in a room. Pictures, ornaments, plants or particular architectural features can all benefit from being in the spotlight. If you prefer natural light effects, flickering candles and firelight will completely change the ambience of the room. They convey a warmth, romanticism and sense of relaxation unlike any other.

LIGHTS AND SWITCHES

Lighting can make a big difference to a room. A bare light bulb swinging from the ceiling not only looks awful, it makes everything else in the room look awful, too. So, before you go any further, see how you can improve the lighting you have. Damaged, tired or faded lampshades should be replaced; even a cheap alternative will improve the look of a room. It may be better to go for a warmer, creamy shade than a white one, which can create a much colder effect. Or you might consider swapping a standard daytime bulb with a warm-toned (red or orange) bulb, which will give a completely different sort of light. Central ceiling lights in a living room or bedroom are never as complimentary or atmospheric as a range of table lamps or a pair of bedside lamps, which are much softer.

DOCTOR'S ORDERS

- **Look at cleaning up existing light fittings before investing in new ones.**
- **If you are going to replace, first define your period.**
- **Decide whether you're going with authentic or repro materials.**
- **Use officially approved lights and fittings.**
- **Ensure that all wiring in your home is sound.**
- **Shop around for your switches and light fittings – the first ones you find are not always the best or the cheapest.**
- **Always use a properly qualified electrician.**

LIGHT FEVER

In the kitchen it's important to ensure that your working areas are adequately lit. Clip-on spotlights or a track of halogen downlighters may be a worthwhile investment. Candlelight can be both flattering and dramatic. Throw out any half-burned stubs and arrange new candles to give some extra atmosphere. Nor is it expensive to replace your switches with dimmers, which give you the advantage of being able to alter the strength of lighting in the room to suit the time of day.

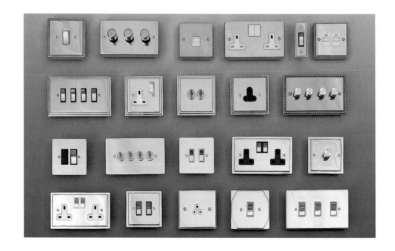

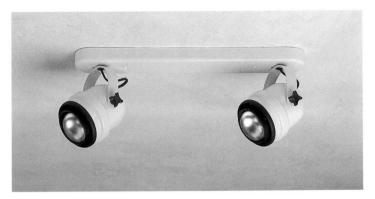

A tracking system of halogen spotlights is ideal for lighting a kitchen.

ABOVE A standard lamp and a table lamp provide useful background lighting.

LEFT Choose your light switches to suit the period and style of your home. There is a huge range to choose from.

An uplighter is a good way of achieving ambient light.

A downlighter is another way of providing ambient light.

SOURCES

CHRISTOPHER WRAY
591–593 Kings Road
London
SW6 2YW
Tel: 020 7751 8701
www.christopherwray.com

ELECTRIC LIGHT COMPANY
Unit 40
Mereview Industrial Estate
Yaxley
Peterborough
PE7 3HS
Tel: 0845 6444 317
www.electriclightcompany.co.uk

THE LIGHTING SUPERSTORE
Unit G11
Avonside Enterprise Park
Melksham
Wiltshire
SN12 8BS
Tel: 01225 704442
www.thelightingsuperstore.co.uk

SCP
135–139 Curtain Road
London
EC2A 3BX
Tel: 020 7739 1869
www.scp.co.uk

WEBSITES
www.easylighting.co.uk
www.lampslighting.co.uk

L

LIVING ROOMS

The living room can show signs of too much life. If potential buyers are going to be able to mentally move their own things in, you've got to make it easy for them by removing too much evidence of yourself and emphasizing the room's potential.

Breathe some fresh air into the room by repainting or repapering it in a warm, but neutral colour. If the carpet's worn or has absorbed the smell of your pets, replace it. Again, a neutral colour is ideal. You can always brighten things up with a rug or two, which can go with you when you move.

Favourite ornaments and family photographs must all be thinned out. If you can move the TV to a more discreet spot, then do so. Put your CD collection into a racking system and weed out your bookshelves. They don't have to be stuffed with books – use them to showcase special ornaments.

Make the most of the focal point in the room. Fireplaces should be swept and mantelpieces cleared of all but a couple of items. If you have a particularly old-fashioned heater, think about replacing it with something more up-to-date. Hang a mirror or picture above the fireplace to emphasize its importance as a feature in the room. A blazing fire always looks welcoming, but empty the grate when it's out. If the room overlooks the garden, frame the windows with curtains and make sure nothing in the room blocks out the view.

There should be easy passage through the room, so check the door isn't obstructed and that French windows are easily accessible. Don't crowd the room with furniture or line it up around the walls – both make the room appear small and unwelcoming. Use the space to its best advantage. Finish with a few well-chosen accessories in your accent colours – cushions, a rug, flowers (real ones), pot-pourri and candles will all help the transformation into a comfortable and desirable room.

L

10 BEST TIPS FOR LIVING ROOMS

1

Pay attention to the windows. Clean them, take away clutter that's obstructing the view and frame them with well-hung curtains or blinds.

2

Make a focal point of the fireplace, a special furniture grouping or even an interesting piece of art.

3

Tidy up the bookshelves. Group books in size order for a feeling of uniformity. To create a sense of space, leave a bit of room for one or two ornaments.

4

Arrange the furniture so that nothing obstructs an easy passage through the room.

5

Good lighting can enhance the space and show off the room at its best.

6

Hide all your family photos, golfing trophies or framed certificates. They only distract the viewers' attention away from the room and prevent them from making the crucial leap of seeing themselves living there.

7

Remove all evidence of pets and children. If that means removing the carpet too, then do it.

8

Hide ugly radiators by boxing them in. This also provides a useful shelf for displaying one or two of your favourite ornaments.

9

Don't forget to add a few finishing touches. Colour and life can be brought into the room by judicious use of cushions, rugs, pictures and flowers. Be careful not to overdo it, though.

10

Having all the furniture lined up around the walls only makes the room look small and unwelcoming.

L

LIVING ROOM TRANSFORMATIONS

DIAGNOSIS

The estate agent had warned me that this sitting room was not presented at its best. Certainly, the first thing I saw when I walked in was an old Christmas tree stuffed behind the sofa and then the general mess – bad Feng Shui all round. The owner had painted the room herself but in a gaudy orange which detracted from the more sophisticated atmosphere that a room like this should possess. And the fireplace was hidden beneath an array of knick-knacks completely covering both shelves. Original features in a period house are almost always deemed selling points so it's wise to show them off. The TV and videos dominated one corner of the room which presented a problem because there was no obvious place to hide them. I wasn't convinced that the rug was doing much for the room either, except making it seem smaller. This was a case of taking the family out before I could put the elegance back in.

Bamboo blinds ensure privacy while letting the light flood into a room.

Candles add to the ambience. New ones are far superior to sad-looking, half-burnt ones.

before

TREATMENT

First, we had to get rid of that ugly orange and repaint with a gentler, more subtle shade. Most importantly though, this room needed a really good clear out – buyers have to be helped to make the mental leap of imagining themselves living somewhere new. The good points of this room were lost under the clutter. Once the mantelpiece was cleared, I made an elegant focal point by adding some candles and a bunch of fresh flowers with a mirror hung above.

I wanted to hide the television, but with no suitable cupboard I decided on a screen. To make this, I hinged together the sides of an inexpensive flat-pack shelving unit and stapled the fabric over them. A simple, but effective solution to covering an eyesore. I had enough fabric left over to cover a small footstool, which helped to unify the room and add colour. In the basement I found some fabulous antique furniture which I moved in here to give the room a more sophisticated, adult look. Peaceful and spacious, it was now seen at its best.

Hide unattractive objects or features behind a simple hand-made screen.

LIVING ROOM TRANSFORMATIONS

before

Dejunk thoroughly. Too much clutter will distract a buyer from seeing the properties of the room.

Unearth forgotten ornaments from your cupboards and showcase them on newly cleared shelves.

DIAGNOSIS

The vivid blue here was overwhelming and did nothing for the room. The same went for the amount of clutter that was crammed in. Result: the living room looked tiny and cramped, giving away more about the owner's lifestyle than one needed to know. The room lacked a focal point and the absence of a dining area was a big minus point. My job was to clearly define the separate areas of the room and neutralize the colours while the owner cleared up the mess.

TREATMENT

First to go were the blue walls, soon painted a soft peach to make the dark room seem larger and lighter. Clutter was attacked with relish. The shelves in the alcove needed drastic thinning out, leaving only one or two striking ornaments. As the TV dominated the room, I had a simple cupboard built to house it, with the two speakers neatly on either side. Now we had a focal point.

Moving the furniture round allowed enough room for a dining area. A small table and two chairs fitted perfectly into the space that was freed between the kitchen and living areas. A clean, ironed tablecloth and a vase of fresh flowers completed the look.

Having cleared the clutter from the whole room, it was possible to see what else was needed to present it in the best possible way. Although we painted the walls, I retained the colour blue as a contrast. The room was tied together by buying some checked cushions, a rug and a coffee table that fitted in with the lighter, more modern feel of the room. Healthy green plants from the local garden centre provided a finishing touch of life and colour.

A TV can dominate a room, so it's a good idea to remove it or hide it away in a cupboard.

after

M

MIRRORS

Mirrors have long been associated with magic and they're a favourite trick in the design world. They can make a small room look bigger and enhance the available light. A dark or small bathroom, for example, can benefit enormously from a large mirror over the basin. Hallways in this country often lack natural light, making them dark and unwelcoming entrances to your home. The addition of a sizeable mirror can brighten things up and add a sense of width to modest entrances. Also, if your living room lacks a focal point then hanging an attractive mirror could be a simple, practical solution.

DOCTOR'S ORDERS

- Hanging a mirror, above a fireplace for example, can help draw attention to a focal point.
- A mirror at the end of a dark hallway can create a sense of light and space.
- If you have an attractive garden, a strategically placed mirror can help bring the outside in.
- A mirror opposite a window can reflect natural light into a dark room.
- Burning candles in front of mirrors can add light and atmosphere to a room.

LEFT A mirror will brighten up a room and positioned carefully will highlight a feature like a fireplace

ABOVE Bathrooms often have minimal natural light, so fitting a choice mirror is essential. Also, we all need a good view of ourselves when carrying out ablutions!

RIGHT A hallway mirror expands the space and is useful for a last-minute check-up before leaving the house.

M

MODERNIZE

Dated décor is a common problem in this country. Often people simply redecorate in the same style or use the time-honoured excuse, 'It was like this when we bought it.' It's actually very easy to drag your property into the 21st century without spending a fortune. The modern look uses clean lines and multi-function rooms to create a sense of light and space. Use bright colours and natural materials, and consider repainting or re-upholstering old furniture. You'll be rewarded with a fresh, modern look.

before

The furniture in this kitchen was very badly positioned.

Focus attention on your table by adding a runner and a potted plant.

CASE NOTES: KITCHEN REVAMP

I didn't feel the owners had done this kitchen justice. It was a big, bright room but it looked dated, and various DIY jobs had been left unfinished: the so-called 'hatch' was just a hole in the wall, the walls weren't completely plastered and the shelves were left unsealed. The furniture was an odd mismatch of church and farmhouse. I felt that the room needed something more contemporary, so I persuaded the owners to splash out on a brand new table and chairs – it entirely changed the feel of the room. The original patterned tablecloth was another old-fashioned element to the kitchen and it had to go. In its place I felt a fabric runner would give focus to that side of the room.

after

NEUTRALIZE

When preparing your property for sale it's important to allow buyers to visualize themselves in your home. Your tastes may be bold and colourful but a buyer needs to feel they can move straight into your house and introduce their own style. They need a blank canvas on which to paint their personality, and the best way to achieve this is to neutralize. Tone down wall colours and floor colourings. Use stronger colours sparingly as accents to create a pleasing colour scheme that runs throughout the house.

before

A grey sofa and orange walls was not a match made in heaven.

after

Fresh white upholstery continued the neutral theme.

CASE NOTES: A LIGHTER SHADE

What a depressing room! Deep orange walls might work well in Mediterranean light, which is strong enough to soften the colour, but in southeast England they are just overbearing. These walls certainly did not allow buyers to envisage the room as a blank canvas. Matters were not helped by the fact that they were large expanses of wall with little to break them up. Painting the walls a pale cream instantly solved the problem, and the colour worked much better with the dark wooden floor. We re-upholstered the sofa in a white fabric to keep things light and installed a new, textured white rug. To break up the walls we added a shelf over the fireplace, a mirror and colour-coordinated wall hangings.

OFFICE AT HOME

With more people working from home all the time and children becoming more reliant on computers for homework, a home office is a huge plus point for any potential buyer. A spare room, attic or even a living room or dining area can double as working environment without losing its primary function. It's important that the dual purposes of the room do not conflict, so simply dumping a computer on a dressing table is a definite no-no. The working area should be clearly defined, preferably with a built-in work station, and complete with appropriate storage and desk space. Work-related clutter such as computer discs, stationary and reference books should be kept tidy in filing systems or storage boxes.

THE WIRELESS OFFICE

Don't let a mess of spaghetti wiring ruin your new look home office or your living room. When you have a lot of electronic equipment in one place – a computer, printer and scanner in an office or a TV, hi-fi and DVD player in a living room – make sure cables are kept tidy. Hide them under carpets and below skirting boards where possible, and invest in some cable tidies for anything that remains on view.

CASE NOTES: DOUBLING UP

This bedroom-cum-office was full to the brim with clutter, making it far from conducive to a good night's sleep. Before anything was done to this room, it had to be thoroughly cleared and cleaned. Once the clutter had been removed, I got rid of the sad-looking brown desk. If a bedroom is to double as an office, then it's wise to build in some furniture that can be used for work and storage, so I installed this modern desk area. There are so many attractive storage boxes and filing systems around that there's no excuse for untidiness.

The lifeless wall colour was changed to a smart blue, which immediately lifted the room and brought it bang up to date. The deliberate absence of pictures contrasted strongly with the room's previous incarnation and now promoted a feeling of calm. The old carpet was taken up and the wooden floor stripped – this is cheaper to do than recarpeting and can look just as good. Bear in mind who's below, though. If the sound of you pacing your workplace isn't muffled by carpet, those underneath may be less than pleased.

before

Keeping all your paperwork tidy
is imperative to an efficient
workspace, especially if the room's
doubling up as another living area.

after

PAINTING

Painting a room can transform its character, but make sure you choose the right colour and finish to give the results you want. Once you've made this decision it's time to think about your technique. Get the right amount of paint on your brush by dipping it into the paint until one-third of the bristles are covered, then pressing it against the paint container. If using a roller, push it backwards and forwards in the paint tray, then up the slope of the tray to get rid of the excess paint. As you work, make sure the paint is 'laid off', or smoothed over, while wet. Remember, two thin coats of paint are better than one thick one. The order in which to paint a room is ceiling, walls, then woodwork.

DOCTOR'S ORDERS

- **Before starting to paint, stack furniture in the centre of the room and cover it with dust sheets.**
- **Ensure windows are open and that you have adequate ventilation.**
- **Mask windows, glasswork and light fittings.**
- **Fill splits in woodwork with wood filler, sanding off the excess.**
- **Paint ceilings first, then walls, then woodwork.**
- **Paint ceilings in strips, working from the window.**
- **Cover large surfaces with a paint roller and use brushes for smaller areas.**
- **Avoid direct draughts on drying paint.**

WHICH FINISH AND COLOUR?

The shiny finishes of gloss, eggshell and vinyl silk reflect light to make a room look larger. Matt finishes, especially in dark colours, will make a room seem smaller. When choosing colours, take into account what furnishings are in the room. Tiny squares of colour on paint charts are not representative of what the colour will look like on all four walls. If possible, paint a large piece of lining paper or MDF and move it around the room so you can see exactly how it looks in different lights at different times of the day. In the cold English light, for example, it is often better to use slightly warmer colours to bring the room to life – off-white or cream is often a better choice than pure white, while soft aquamarines, eau de nil, peaches and apricots are preferable to bright blues or oranges. Also look at the proposed colour during different times of the day and under artificial light. Think about when the room is used most often and judge whether or not this is when the colour looks its best.

PREPARATION AND TECHNIQUES

Make sure all odd jobs are completed before you commence painting. Fixing a sash cord or broken door or light switch later may well mess up your finished paintwork. Remove furniture or stack it in the centre and cover with a dustsheet. Ensure the surfaces to be painted are clean and carefully prepared, repairing any damage such as blisters, flaking paint, chips and cracks. You're now ready to paint different areas of a room:

Ceiling If using a brush, begin in a corner then work in strips away from the light. If using a roller, first paint the tricky corners with a small brush then roller the main area with alternating diagonal strokes.

Woodwork For a flat-surfaced door, paint from top to bottom in strips For a panelled door, paint the panels first, then the sections between them. Finish off with the top, bottom, then sides of the door.

Windows Apply masking tape to the edges of windows and begin painting the sections nearest the glass, working outwards to paint the window frame last. Pull the top of a sash window down and the bottom up before painting.

Walls Start at the top corner, working in strips down to the skirting board, then returning to the top. Use a smaller brush to 'cut in' around the doors and windows. A roller should be used in alternating diagonal strokes so that gaps are merged. Try to paint an entire wall while working in the same light so that you can see where you have covered.

The colour you paint a room can profoundly influence mood – white is clean, calming and peaceful.

SEE ALSO

Colour	p36
Colour schemes	p38

P

PATTERN

Once you have prepared your home for sale by neutralizing the property, it's important to introduce colour and pattern in moderation. Clever use of patterns can add interest to a room and create all-important visual stimulation. Certain patterns are useful for tricking the eye – for example, vertically striped wallpaper can help make a low ceiling feel higher. Repeating and coordinating patterns in fabric, cushions and curtains can help tie a design scheme together. But be careful not to use too many loud or clashing patterns, particularly on large areas like walls and floors. These can make a room feel cluttered and claustrophobic.

WICKED WALLS

Wallpaper design has come a long way since the floral nightmares of previous decades. These days interesting and exciting patterns are readily available and they can add style and bring a new dimension to your home. Take your time and think carefully about your design; consider limiting your stylish new pattern to a small area, such as an accent wall. You'll then be able to continue the pattern through rugs, soft furnishings and accessories.

The limited use of pattern in an otherwise neutral room can make an impact without being overpowering. The matching drapes and cushion add subtle accents of pattern that tie together different elements in the room.

CASE NOTES: PLAGUE OF PATTERNS

In this living room patterns had been allowed to run riot, with floral wallpaper and unmatched floral curtains, a heavily figured carpet, and to cap it all a swirly ceiling. Anything that moved had a pattern, and except for the curtains and a solitary cushion, none of them matched or lived happily side by side; on the contrary, they fought like cat and dog. This plethora of patterns, together with the dark, oversized furniture and dark wood, made this small room seem minuscule.

Some radical changes were needed to make the room feel brighter and more spacious. We painted the wallpaper a clean cream, laid a neutral carpet and replaced the old floral curtains – not with a neutral fabric but with a cheerful red gingham. Using pattern in a limited way like this is much more effective and means it can actually be appreciated.

before

after

PERIOD FEATURES

Many British homes have beautiful period features but it's surprising how many of you fail to make the most of them. I've seen stunning period fireplaces blocked by ugly, old armchairs or original mosaic floors covered with threadbare carpet. Period features are loved by buyers. They include dado rails, original fireplaces, cornicing and other decorative plasterwork inside the house and tiled paths and period front-doors outside. These are selling points – they should be on view and, what's more, they should be focal points. Original plasterwork should be clean and freshly painted. Make sure your period fireplace isn't crowded by furniture or cluttered with ornaments. It should be clean, with tiles regrouted and cast-iron work repolished with graphite paste.

DOCTOR'S ORDERS

- Check the style of your doors – both internal and external – is in keeping with the period of your house.
- If original period features have been removed, consider fitting a repro feature that matches the style and period of the house.
- Period features have often been covered up by previous owners desperate to modernize. If you live in an old house, check what lies beneath that yucky seventies' fireplace or boring carpet.
- Keep period features clean and well maintained.

CASE NOTES: BEST FEATURES

The wallpaper in this bedroom took my breath away. It was essential that we toned it down so that any potential buyer could consider the merits of the room uninterrupted. The owners had decided to box in the hole left when the original fireplace was removed and paper over it. A big mistake, in my view. Most people want as many original features as possible when they are buying a period home. It's almost always advisable to restore or replace them if you can. The bed looked as if it had been made in a hurry and the amount of clutter made the room feel claustrophobic and cramped.

Unlike in the early days of central heating when redundant fireplaces were boxed in, now they are appreciated for their period worth. Not only that, but they provide a wonderful focal point to a room whether or not they're used. Before redecorating, we removed the box that hid the hole where the fireplace had once been. We found an appropriate Victorian fireplace with surround in an architectural salvage yard. Painted white, it completely transformed the feel of the room, giving it an elegance that had previously been missing.

before

The fireplace surround gave the room some definite lines and brought some much-needed character to the space.

after

P

PETS

You guys are renowned as a nation of animal lovers but that's not much use when it comes to selling houses. The dog may be man's best friend but he's a buyer's worst enemy. From cats to cockatiels, bunnies to budgies, the odour of your critters is sure to have a buyer turning their nose up at your property. Ideally you would pack off your pooches until your house has sold, and if you share your home with a dangerous animal, sometimes that's the only option. However, if your pets are going to stay you need to remove all traces of their hair and odour before buyers arrive, and make sure the garden is clear of toys, chewed bones and any other 'little presents' your animals may have left behind.

DOCTOR'S ORDERS

- Prevent pets from lying on furniture.
- If they do, cover furniture with washable, removable covers or throws.
- Disguise pet smells with natural air fresheners such as pot-pourri and fresh flowers or plants.
- Vacuum furniture and carpets to remove all traces of pet hair.
- Keep animals away from kitchen or dining areas at all times.
- Limit your pet's domain – if possible to the garden or conservatory.
- Tend to your pets – clean, well-groomed animals shed less hair and smell better.

RIGHT The ultimate pet sin –
keeping one in a bathroom.
And even worse, it's a rat!

BELOW A dog or cat can provide
love and affection in the home, but
regularly vacuum the areas where
they roam.

OPPOSITE Allowing pets into
the bedroom is never a good
idea, especially if you suffer
from allergies.

PLANTS AND FLOWERS

Plants and flowers can add life, colour and contrast to a room, but only if they are healthy and displayed well. Unless you are blessed with green fingers, it is wise to choose plants that will withstand almost any amount of neglect. Take advice from the local garden centre. When choosing a plant, make sure that it looks healthy, that roots are not coming out of the pot's drainage holes and that there is no moss or slime on the compost.

You don't have to go over the top with household foliage – one well-chosen plant will do the trick.

CARING FOR PLANTS

Houseplants come in all shapes and sizes to suit almost any situation. The rules of thumb when caring for indoor plants are: put them where they will thrive best, not only where they look best; water and feed them according to instructions; treat any disease or pest the moment you spot it; avoid extremes of cold and heat; trim off dead flowers and leaves; and if a plant begins to look as if it is suffering, ask yourself why it is suffering and remedy it. Find out what conditions your plants experience in the wild and try to imitate them as closely as possible.

CHOOSING CONTAINERS

There is no limit to the type of containers suitable for houseplants. There is no reason why you can't use decorative tins, seaside buckets, teapots, glass containers or even an old butler's sink. The most common container, of course, is the tried-and-tested terracotta pot, which goes well with any plant and allows moisture to evaporate through its sides. Such pots can be used alone or placed inside a cache-pot whose design suits the décor better. Groups of plants can make an attractive feature or focal point in a room. They may be freestanding, or smaller arrangements will fit into terrariums, bottle gardens or a trough. Window boxes do not have to be restricted to the outside of the house. If there's no sill or they are in danger of falling, try bringing them inside. They may be ideal for growing herbs or small flowering border plants.

Use your imagination to find ways of using plants to enhance a space, be it dramatic, exotic, soothing or just plain welcoming. Remember, a few well chosen, well cared-for plants are an asset to any décor; an overgrown jungle is a definite liability.

WHAT PLANT GOES WHERE?

Small, bushy flowering pot plants such as chrysanthemums, azaleas or cyclamen make good seasonal centrepieces for tables, and will also sit happily on a mantelpiece or windowsill. Trailing plants such as the spider plant, sweetheart plant, wandering Jew or devil's ivy can sit on a plant stand, shelf or wall bracket and cascade downwards. If placed near a window, they can be used to hide an unappealing view. Exotic palms make grand statements, and are suitable for both a modern environment and a more traditional room. They will live happily in living or dining rooms where the temperature remains reasonably constant.

If you want to put greenery into your bathroom, try one of the ferns. They love a warm humid environment, so if the bathroom doesn't steam up often, make sure you spray them regularly. Kitchens are generally not a great home for plants because of the fluctuating temperature. But if you insist, it's best to go for the real death-defying specimens such as peace lilies, sweetheart plants, mother-in-law's tongues, devil's ivy or umbrella plants. If you just want something small on the window ledge, try growing your own herbs.

TOP Cheap and very cheerful, tulips are available in a wide range of colours.

ABOVE Household plants with leaves that drop off need to be regularly maintained.

QUAINT

In my experience, there's one very British word that constantly crops up as an excuse for shocking décor, and that's 'quaint'. Your hideous floral wallpaper may indeed be quaint but it's also quite disgusting. Your chintzy furniture and frilly curtains should have stayed where they belong – in the past. If your property falls into the 'quaint' category, it's time to bring it back to the future. That means losing the 'little old lady' look, deflowering those walls and repainting in modern, neutral colours.

before

CASE NOTES: SHOCKING PINK

This really was quaint in the worst sense of the word. The carpet was far too swirly and pink for any prospective buyer and the walls incorporated ornate stencilling which had been lovingly put up by the owner. The heavily patterned carpet was the first thing to go, replaced by a chic new beige-coloured substitute. The walls were painted a soft, clean colour to obliterate the pinks and I even allowed a new border to be put up, though it was much more discreet than the original one. Finally, some of the artwork in the original room could also have been described as quaint and in its place went something more innocuous.

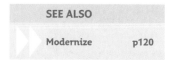

SEE ALSO

Modernize   p120

after

RADIATORS

Radiators are more than just practical objects that generate heat. They can also make a design statement, so if your budget allows, consider investing in one of the many different types on the market. On a practical level, make sure that the radiators are working and the house is warm in the winter. Don't block them with furniture or curtains. If you have standard functional wall fittings which add nothing to a room, think about boxing them in – it's a simple job. If the paintwork is chipped or you want to make more or less of a feature of them, there is a wide range of specialist radiator paints available.

ABOVE By boxing in a radiator you can add a simple design feature and a practical shelf.

LEFT There is a wide range of radiator styles available, from reclaimed Victorian examples to contemporary designs.

SOURCES

CARADON PLUMBING LTD
Lawton Road
Alsager
Stoke-on-Trent
ST7 2DF
Tel: 0870 840100

PREMIER RADIATOR COVERS
Unit 2
Mountain Ash Ind. Estate
Mountain Ash
Mid Glamorgan
CF45 4EY
Tel: 01443 477824

THE RADIATOR CENTRE
2 Grand Parade
Polegate
East Sussex
BN26 5HG
Tel: 01323 486848
www.wpah.co.uk

FEATURE RADIATORS
Bingley Railway Station
Wellington Street
Bingley
West Yorkshire
BD16 2NB
Tel: 01274 567789
www.featureradiators.co.uk

WEBSITES
www.rads.uk.com
www.designer-radiators.com

S

SHELVING

Shelving is a great way to keep clutter neatly stored and to display favourite ornaments. Various shelving options are available – free standing, wall mounted, built in – so there shouldn't be any need for the overcrowding that seems to occur on many of your shelves or bookcases. Overcrowding gives the impression that there isn't enough storage space in the room, and if you intend to sell your property, this will immediately put off prospective buyers. If you have an empty alcove, put up inexpensive laminate shelving to provide both storage and display space. Ornaments can also be used to break up shelf space, making it look bigger.

DOCTOR'S ORDERS

- **Make a rough sketch and plan your storage.**
- **Consider the weight and height of what you intend to store on the shelf.**
- **Thin shelves will sag if heavily laden unless they are well supported.**
- **Aim to keep everyday items within easy reach.**
- **Allow sufficient clearance so that books or other items can be easily removed and returned.**
- **Consider whether you would be better off with adjustable shelving.**
- **Use a spirit level to make sure shelves are level.**

CASE NOTES: A LONGER SHELF LIFE

The messages given by this room were muddled. The Victorian fireplace sat uneasily beside the modern shelves and furniture. And although it's said that books furnish a room, they're not the only things that look good on shelves – there were just far too many of them. Weeding them out would give more emphasis to the fireplace.

before

after

The junk was moved from the shelves and mantelpiece, allowing the room to breathe. A new colour scheme dramatically altered the whole feel, making it more up-to-date and appealing. To underline the contemporary style of the room, accessories for the shelves were chosen especially to tone in with the colour scheme. But the Victorian fire surround didn't fit in with the new look. So specialist paints were used to hide the tiles and transform the whole thing into a modern fireplace that blended with the overall look of the room.

SEE ALSO

| Display | p58 |
| Storage | p142 |

SMALL SPACES

Small spaces can often be the biggest headache. When planning your design for small rooms or bedsits, it's important to make use of all available space. That means plenty of shelving and storage, particularly in any dead areas like alcoves. Make use of dual-function furniture, like sofabeds, seating that doubles as storage, or dining tables that can convert into desks. Explore all available storage options and utilize awkward spaces such as under stairs. Paint in neutral colours to make the area feel more spacious and make clever use of mirrors to add the illusion of space.

DOCTOR'S ORDERS

- **Ensure furniture is not too big for the room.**
- **Keep small spaces free from any clutter.**
- **Make sure windows are clean and are not blocked by curtains or objects positioned in front of them.**
- **Use uplighters to exaggerate the height of a ceiling.**
- **Use mirrors to reflect both natural and artificial light. Place them opposite a window, behind candles or above a fireplace – reflected light can help to increase the proportions of a room.**
- **Choose materials, furniture and objects that reflect light, such as glass, metal, polished wood, silky fabrics and gloss and silk paints.**

ABOVE Clever storage ideas such as this curtained wardrobe are essential if small spaces are to both function well and look good.

LEFT A small kitchen needs extremely careful planning if it is to work well. Make sure that all drawers, cupboards and appliances are easily accessible.

SEE ALSO

Colour	p36
Painting	p124
Storage	p142

LEFT With careful planning, this 'dead' space under the stairs has been converted into a workstation.

BELOW Make the most of a small room by decorating it simply, in plain or neutral colours, and using a few items of furniture that suit the room's scale. A mirror will increase the light and deepen the space.

S

STAGING

What is this novel new concept that I bring with me from the United States? It is called 'home staging', and has become hugely successful in my home state of California. Simply put, home staging is a manner of presenting a home for sale so that it will appeal to the broadest buying audience, 'setting the stage' as it were, so that when the ready, willing and able buyer walks through the door, they are immediately hooked. There is nothing here that is dishonest in any way, and no trickery is involved. It is a simple technique that makes the most of what your home already has, thus allowing prospective buyers to see it in its most favourable light and – more importantly – to see themselves living there. Home staging enables a buyer to mentally 'move in' to your home.

Staging could simply be adding a classy vase and a few tasteful magazines to a coffee table.

A PROCESS OF REFINEMENT

Staging is an editing process. Everything personal, unnecessary or extreme is removed from the home and replaced with things that have a neutral, minimal and harmonious feel to them (whereas much interior design is a supplementing process; its goal is to surround the client with beautiful things that have a personal meaning to them as individuals). Staging is done with no one in particular in mind (or rather, with everyone in particular in mind), and in a staging project, no matter what the asking price of the home, the object is to spend as little money as possible to get the expected result. I try to use a lot of what the client already owns, arrange it differently and spend money only on essentials, most of which the client can take with them when they move. I always reserve the last bit of cash for things like fresh flowers, cheery plants, fluffy new towels, colourful cushions, scented soaps and pot-pourri – those little extras that cost almost nothing, but give the impression of freshness and attention to detail. The entire environment is 'staged' to give positive subliminal suggestions to prospective buyers, in much the same way as in the world of advertising.

S

STORAGE

Storage is a buzzword in contemporary design. It's true that you can't have enough storage space in a house. And if you're thinking of selling, it's one of the things that your potential buyers will definitely look out for. You may be happy living in a relaxed family home with things piled up on every surface, but they may be of a more minimalist bent and will want assurance that their belongings can be stored. If you leave everything out, it gives the impression that the house is too small and doesn't have enough space in which to keep it. You can rectify this easily by the addition of some simple storage ideas.

DOCTOR'S ORDERS

- Alcoves on either side of the chimney breast are an ideal place for shelves.
- Stuff children's toys into large plastic boxes.
- Self-assembly drawers will slip neatly under a bed.
- Open shelves in a kitchen are great for storage and don't make the room appear smaller.
- Glass shelves work brilliantly in a bathroom and even sometimes across windows.
- Shelves don't have to be used for books – ornaments can look good, too.
- Make sure all cupboard doors shut properly so they don't look as if they're literally stuffed to bursting.

STORAGE SYSTEMS

Obviously this is not the moment to build fitted cupboards but you'll find inexpensive storage systems in your local department store or DIY shop, not to mention the specialist shops that have sprung up recently. CD, DVD and video collections should be found a home off the floor. Books should be thinned out and neatly shelved. In one house I staged, we used a third bedroom specifically as a dressing room where all the jumble from the master bedroom was neatly sorted and stored. You will be able to lay your hands on all shapes and sizes of boxes to hold photos, papers and other essential bits and pieces. Canvas wardrobes, fabric shoe-holders, wine racks and mobile kitchen units are only a few of the ideas that await you. If your budget won't allow the investment, then use your attic, below-stairs space and, if the worst really comes to the worst, the boot of your car!

SEE ALSO

| Clutter | p34 |
| Shelving | p136 |

These boxes could be used to hide away almost anything.

Shoes can be a nightmare to keep tidy. A handy shoe rack makes all the difference.

Better to hang clothes up than leave them slung over the bedroom furniture.

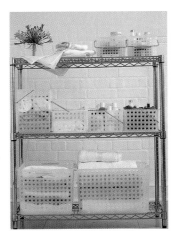

All sorts of things, from clothes to toiletries, can be neatly stored in mesh boxes on a shelving system.

A simple racking system can help tidy up a bathroom or kitchen.

SOURCES

THE HOLDING COMPANY
Burlington House
184 New Kings Road
London
SW6 4NF
Tel: 020 7610 9160
www.theholdingcompany.co.uk

HABITAT UK LTD
196 Tottenham Court Road
London
W1T 7LG
Tel: 020 7631 3880
www.habitat.co.uk

IKEA LTD
Croydon
Tel: 0845 355 1144
Leeds
Tel: 0845 355 2261
Glasgow
Tel: 0845 355 2266
www.ikea.co.uk

LAURA ASHLEY
PO Box 19
Newtown
Powys
SY16 1DZ
Tel: 0871 9835 999
www.lauraashley.com

WEBSITES
www.oceanuk.com
www.pier.co.uk

TILES

Ceramic tiles are one of the most hygienic and durable surfaces in the home, but if they aren't kept spotlessly clean, they can look very scruffy. And if you are selling, that's an immediate turn off for a prospective buyer. That means clean, clean and clean again. Use warm soapy water, a scrubbing brush and plenty of elbow grease. If that fails, regrouting or painting existing grouting with a specialist grout-painting pen can give your tiles a new lease of life. If tiles themselves are stained, dated or just plain ugly, there are a number of specialist tile paints that will instantly transform them.

TOP Colourful tiles have the ability to bring an area to life and become a feature in themselves.

LEFT Tiling provides a hygienic, hard-wearing surface that is ideal for bathrooms.

ABOVE Clean, white tiles in a bathroom are an inexpensive way of freshening up the space.

SOURCES

CERAMIC PRINTS
George Street
Brighouse
Yorkshire
HD6 1PU
01484 727 1476
www.ceramicprints.com

TAYLORS TILES
Beaufort Road
Plasmarl
Swansea
SA6 8JG
Tel: 01792 797712
www.taylorstiles.co.uk

WALLS AND FLOORS
Wilson Terrace
Kettering
Northamptonshire
NN16 9RT
Tel: 01536 410484
www.wallsandfloors.co.uk

WORLD'S END TILES
Silverthorne Road
London
SW8 3HE
Tel: 020 7819 2110
www.worldsedtiles.co.uk

WEBSITES
www.domustiles.com
www.reedharris.co.uk
www.tilesofstow.co.uk

TRICKS OF THE TRADE

If you want to sell your home, preparing it isn't rocket science, but it helps to have a checklist handy before inviting buyers through your front door. There are a number of things to get right if you're going to tempt them into making an offer, and, equally, there are plenty of mistakes which will send a buyer running for cover. If you follow my list of 'dos' and 'don'ts', you should be well on the way to a successful sale.

TOP 10 THINGS TO DO

1 **Neutralize** Tone down your wall colours and floor colourings to provide a clean, blank canvas. Use stronger colours sparingly.

2 **Depersonalize** Hide family photos – buyers won't want to be distracted by your life.

3 **Declutter** Tidy up EVERY room. Pack up and store everything that you do not use regularly.

4 **Clean, clean, and clean again** No one wants to live with another person's dirt, so clean like you've never cleaned before.

5 **Check your kerb appeal** The outside of your house is as important as the inside.

6 **Keep your pets under control** Confine them to a specific area while you are selling.

7 **Define each room or area** You're selling a lifestyle, so make sure your buyer is clear where they can entertain, dine, study or play.

8 **DIY now** Finish off all those little jobs, or it may hint that you have left other things unfinished.

9 **Ensure your lighting is sufficient** If necessary, change bulbs to brighter ones or invest in some new light fittings.

10 **Accessorize** Use mirrors to maximize light and space, use splashes of colour, and don't forget plants, fresh flowers and fragrances.

TOP 10 THINGS NOT TO DO

1 **Carpet your bathroom** Bathroom carpets hold moisture, look drab and can smell.

2 **Paint the walls in garish colours** Your buyer may find them overwhelming and they often make a room seem smaller and darker.

3 **Forget to wash up** Do the washing up the night before and put it all away.

4 **Leave the TV or blaring music on** It's distracting. I sometimes hide the television by putting it in a cupboard or behind a screen.

5 **Leave beds unmade or clothing in piles** No one wants to see your 'dirty laundry'.

6 **Believe other people are like you** Buyers should be able to imagine themselves surrounded by their own things, not yours.

7 **Raise red flags in the buyer's mind** Attend to things like damp patches and stained ceilings, which hint at bigger problems.

8 **Block the views** Make the most of views by clearing clutter from window ledges, polishing windows and putting up curtains.

9 **Have the house too warm or cold** A buyer needs to feel comfortable when viewing.

10 **Engage in lengthy chatter with viewers** Leave that to your estate agent.

UNFINISHED BUSINESS

Remember all those little jobs around the house that you've always meant to finish? Now's the time to do them. If the delay has been because you don't really know what you're doing, then get someone in who does. It won't be expensive and it's vital if you're selling your house. Broken window catches, a door bell that doesn't work or half-finished shelves convey an air of neglect and send out the wrong signals to a potential buyer.

before

after

The split-cane blind was shabby and did the room no favours at all. I replaced it with a lighter one and also added curtains.

CASE NOTES: COMPLETING THE JOB

The diagnosis was straightforward enough: the bedroom had never been finished. There was a marked air of general neglect and the room left too many question marks in a viewer's mind. Leaking roof? Damp? The window and fireplace were prime candidates for making into focal points. And the unpleasant-looking bedding and star light-shade had to go before an injection of life began and the room was given focus.

The walls were painted a soft apple green. The paper lantern was replaced by a toning green shade, and, using the bedspread as the basis for other colours, I chose scatter cushions and a throw to disguise the old blue sofa. I turned the bed to face the fireplace, and added a chest of drawers and bookshelf to suggest the room had storage space.

UPHOLSTERY

Tired old sofas and armchairs that look as if they've lost their bounce can be brought back to life fairly simply and inexpensively. You can add cushions or throws or even re-upholster the chairs you have. When choosing new fabric, remember what else is in the room when you look at different textures, colours and patterns. If you are unsure, it is often wise to go for a neutral colour, relying on its texture for interest. Then, when it's in situ, dress it up with a coloured cushion or two that will tie it in with the general colour scheme.

CUSHIONS

Cushions come in limitless sizes and shapes and are useful for introducing colour, texture and a feeling of comfort to a room. They can coordinate or contrast with the other surfaces and colours in the room and can be used to inject a bit of zip into a depressed piece of furniture. If it's simply a question of your sofa looking neglected, have it professionally cleaned and add some contrasting cushions – it will have a marked effect on the room for very little cost.

LEFT A throw can reinvigorate a worn sofa or armchair. But make sure you choose one that is large enough to cover the whole piece.

OPPOSITE Scatter cushions are versatile items of soft upholstery because they can be moved from one room to another.

COVER-UP JOB

If a more drastic cover-up is needed, the easiest thing is to cover either a sofa or an armchair with a throw. There is a large range of designs and colours available to transform not only the furniture but the whole look of a room. If you don't want to go to the expense of buying a throw, good alternatives are bedspreads, rugs, antique and modern shawls. All of these have the advantage of protecting the sofa from further damage, disguising the damage that has already been done and introducing colour and texture into a room. A disadvantage is the way they will slip untidily out of place unless firmly secured.

A throw can be simply draped over the piece of furniture and held in place by cushions. Greater security is achieved by tucking it into the sides and back of the sofa. To make sure your throw is big enough to do this, measure the sofa from front to back, adding at least another 30cm (12in) to accommodate the tuck, and from side to side, adding another 60cm (24in). Don't skimp. Alternatively, use one throw for the back of the sofa, another for the seat and others over the arms. Small, specialist spiral pins are sold to hold throws in place.

U

UPHOLSTERY

TAILOR-MADE COVERINGS

A more expensive solution is to make or buy loose covers. They will give your sofa or chair a new look at less cost than buying a new one. Try and stick to medium-weight fabrics and, if the covers are washable, check they are shrinkproof. To look their best they need to be carefully measured and fitted, although if you are lucky you may find the perfect off-the-peg solution.

Dining-room chairs can also be given a new lease of life. If they are wooden, they can be touched up with woodstain and varnish, or painted. For colour and comfort add cushions, perhaps even with ties to fasten to the chairback and legs. If the seat is removable, a new cover is the answer. It's easy to remove the seat, lay it upside down on a new piece of fabric, then pull the fabric taut over the top and tack or staple it in place underneath, carefully pleating the corners before covering the base with a piece of plain, tough fabric.

A more dramatic solution is to fit a slip-over cover that reaches to just below the seat or the floor. Made up from a pattern of squares and rectangles, a simple slipcover may have inverted pleats over each leg, button-up backs or tied sides or back.

ABOVE With only a little effort, tables and chairs can be fitted with a fabric covering of your choice.

RIGHT This revamped footstool introduces a note of colour that complements the traditional décor.

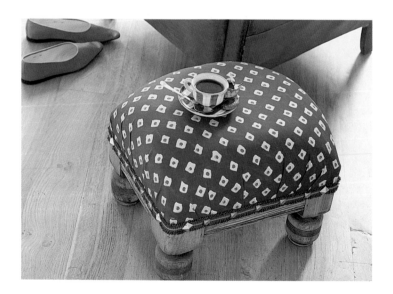

V

VIEWER'S CHECKLIST

If you're selling your home, you're quite likely to be buying a new one to move in to. With this in mind, I think it's worth providing a few tips to help you make sure that it's the right one for you, as well as reminding you how buyers may be researching your own home. Ultimately, when choosing a property, it must feel like it could become your home.

PROPERTY POINTERS

- **Is it for you?** Mentally strip the house of its furniture and look at the space itself, imagining how it will suit your kind of lifestyle and possessions.
- **Structure** Look for any red flags that might suggest something more sinister is wrong with the house. Check for signs of damp, cracks, mould, subsidence – anything unusual that catches your eye.
- **Fittings** Look at the floors and windows, and ensure they don't need replacing.
- **Major repairs** Ascertain whether you will have to refit the bathroom or the kitchen, that the wiring is sound and that the central heating system works properly. All these things are expensive to replace.
- **Space** Check there's space for any particular fittings or appliances you may have.
- **Storage** Ensure there will be room for your larger items of furniture and enough storage and cupboard space.
- **Hidden extras** Look underneath carpets to see the flooring beneath. If you envisage having stripped floorboards, you will be disappointed later to discover concrete slab.

- **Ask the experts** Get a professional to check the structure of the house and have a lawyer check the deeds, conduct a local authority search and administrate your acquisition.
- **Take a second look** Visit the property at different times of the day to see if it's affected by traffic, local noise or fumes.
- **Check the boundaries** Get a lawyer to check the boundaries of the property are exactly those described in the particulars.
- **Get to know the area** Sound out the facilities that may be relevant to you – schools, amenities, future development plans.
- **Talk to the neighbours** Get a real sense of the neighbourhood, then weigh up the positive aspects against the negative ones.
- **On the up?** Find out whether the area is on the up or has peaked. If you're not planning on living there for long, this is important.
- **Why is it for sale?** Find out why the owners are selling. Chances are if they can't live with the loud music, you won't be able to either.
- **Is the price right?** Check what prices other properties have sold for in the area so you can gauge whether or not your price is right.

VIEWS AND VISTAS

If you plan on selling your home, it makes sense to draw a buyer's eye towards the most impressive areas of your property. Likewise, there are myriad ways to hide a bad view. If you have a beautiful garden then a cleverly placed mirror can help bring the outside in. Also, dress your windows to frame, rather than block, a beautiful view. If the scene from your living room window is nothing special, you may prefer to cover it up. Don't use net curtains; choose instead fine fabrics, such as muslins, voiles or unlined cotton.

Simple roller blinds provide privacy while still allowing light through.

SEE ALSO

Curtains and blinds p44
Windows   p155

BLINDS AND SHUTTERS

Blinds are another good investment. Slatted Venetian blinds come in wood, metal or plastic in different colours and widths. Pulled down, the slats can be angled to control the amount of light flowing into a room. Their only disadvantage is that they can be awkward to clean. Plain roller blinds and Roman blinds can be made with fabrics that filter light and screen an unattractive view. Split-cane and bamboo blinds will add a rather colonial feel and look wonderful with the sun streaming through them.

Vertical louvre blinds are attached to the top and bottom of the window. Usually made of strips of canvas or wood, they pivot open and shut and pull open to the side. Café blinds or curtains cover only the lower half of a window, letting in light above them. Similarly, a type of roller blind can be fitted that rolls up from the bottom of the window. These can be pulled up to the right height to hide the view. Added interest can be given to a bay window by raising adjacent blinds to different heights. Louvred shutters are an alternative. They can be divided so that privacy is retained by shutting only the lower half.

USING GLASS

Glass shelving can be fixed across a window and used to hold plants or ornaments, although this makes opening the window difficult, so ensure that it is not a window that you use often. These shelves will successfully obstruct the view, but light will still find its way in around them to provide you with a pleasing natural light effect.

Frosted glass is often used in windows where privacy is particularly desired. If you want the effect without the cost, use a frosting spray.

LEFT Frosted film can be stuck onto windows to achieve a frosted-glass effect. Shapes or patterns cut out of it provide additional interest.

BELOW Make the most of any great view you might have by framing it; these curtains, for example, make a bold statement.

Having cleaned the windows thoroughly, the spray can be used to cover an entire pane or you might stencil a clear line around the edge of the window or patterns in the centre. Frosted film is another possibility. Stuck onto the window, it provides the same effect as frosted glass. For additional interest, or to admit more light, shapes or patterns can be cut out of it.

Churches are not the only preserve of stained or coloured glass. There are modern designs that lend themselves to domestic use. Subtle marbled patterns make a feature of a window while hiding what is behind. Coloured acetate makes a cheap and cheerful alternative. Again, a drawing on tracing paper can be an effective answer. If your room looks onto a brick wall allowing little or no light to come in, paint the wall a bright colour or paint a design or a mural on it to provide something interesting to look at.

WASTED SPACE

With storage facilities one of the first things a buyer looks for in a potential home, you can't afford to waste a single nook or cranny in your property. These days there are a range of innovative storage options to fit all kinds of strange spaces – under stairs, in alcoves or in corners. Remember to take careful measurements of the area before you go shopping. Alternatively, consider putting your DIY skills to the test and building furniture to fit – it's amazing what you can put together with just a few pieces of wood.

This dead space in the corner of a hallway has been transformed by the addition of a zinc corner table. As well as a table to accommodate a telephone and notepad, it doubles up as a useful storage bin.

SEE ALSO

▶▶ Small spaces   p138
Storage   p142

WINDOWS

Windows come in a multitude of styles and can be as bold or understated as you like. If any of your windows are beyond repair, you should replace them – it will make a big difference to your home. Whatever you do, make sure that the replacements are as close to the originals as possible. However, it is more likely that what you will be faced with is some minor repairs. All the paintwork should be touched up where necessary and washed where not. On the exterior of the house, it is safest to go for clean, white gloss on the window frames, making sure that all the windows open and close properly. They can be decorated by using window boxes, provided they are well-planted and colourful. Make sure any curtains or blinds you can see from outside are clean and properly hung.

DRESSING YOUR WINDOWS

When staging a house, it's important to look outside 'the box', too. If there's a particularly good view then draw attention to it by dressing the appropriate window. Curtains don't need to be expensive or elaborate to be effective and they can add colour to the room. Make sure they blend with the general scheme and draw back to let in as much light as possible. Try not to hide the shape of an unusual and attractively designed window. Shabby old net curtains are one of my pet hates. If you want to retain privacy and light, the best solution is to invest in blinds. Venetian blinds are one effective choice, but Roman blinds can be made in fine cotton or voile, which are more feminine and play the same trick. If the view's dire, you might want a curtain which covers the bottom half of the window only.

SEE ALSO
Curtains and blinds p44
Views and vistas   p152

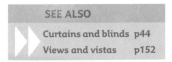

ABOVE Stained or patterned glass can be a cheap, effective way of beautifying an entrance.

LEFT Leaded glass should always be clean to allow the maximum possible light to enter your home.

WINDOWS

RIGHT Doors through to a conservatory should be cleaned on a regular basis.

BELOW RIGHT Glass doors leading to the garden must also be kept spotlessly clean. It's important not to block access to them.

DOCTOR'S ORDERS

- Clean all windows until they sparkle.
- Wash the paintwork around them.
- Ensure that they all open and shut properly.
- Check that all window furniture matches and works.
- Investigate the different kinds of blinds available on the market.
- Don't block the flow of sunlight into the room.

X-FACTOR

If you've ever wondered why some houses are snapped up before the 'For Sale' sign even goes up, while others sit on the market for many months, the answer may lie in what I call the X-factor. This is what makes your house exciting, vibrant and beautiful to look at. It can't be narrowed down to one particular element, but is a combination of little things – plants, flowers and beautiful accessories; the simple reupholstering of a chair cushion or the addition of a stylish rug. Don't forget those final flourishes outside either: put welcoming plants in place to complete the transformation. These tiny touches should be evident all around your home, and should coordinate in perfect harmony. That's what buyers are looking for, and if you get it right then X marks the spot.

ABOVE The simple positioning of pictures and ornaments in the right places can initiate the X-factor.

LEFT The lack of clutter and effective colour coordination in this bedroom create an enticing feel for a potential buyer.

YUK

As a house doctor there have been numerous occasions when I've looked at a property and asked 'why?' Why have you let this place get so yucky? Carpets that stink of cats – yuk! In your face, nightmare-inducing colours – yuk! Grubby, garish hallways from hell – yuk! Buyers aren't impressed by the yuk factor, but thankfully, with a little cleaning, neutralizing and a properly coordinating colour scheme, you can quickly transform your home from yuk to yum.

ABOVE Does this hideous bathroom really need an explanation as to why it's yuk?

RIGHT Mountains of clutter hint at festering uncleanliness and that is, quite simply, yuk.

Z

ZODIAC

You will know by now that the secrets of successful design are written in this book; however, they may also be written in the stars. Without wanting to be too hippy about it, let's take a look at how the zodiac could offer some design inspiration. Air signs like Gemini, Libra and Aquarius tend towards the artistic, the innovative and the original. Their designs are lively and rarely boring, but they are sometimes overbearing. Fire houses, Aries, Leo and Sagittarius have strong, confident designs with in-your-face colour, serious glitz and glamour and the threat of OTT décor. Sensitive water signs, like Cancer, Scorpio or Pisces, will often incorporate the mystical, or perhaps indulge their signs' sense of passion with some daring detail. And finally earth signs Taurus, Virgo and Capricorn are traditional, down to earth and a little eccentric. True Brits in fact. Expect twin sets and teapots in a no-nonsense, occasionally untidy setting.

The bold reds in this room suggest that the owner of the property was born under a fire sign.

ACKNOWLEDGEMENTS

AUTHOR ACKNOWLEDGEMENTS

I would like to thank Cat Ledger, Five TV, Talkback Productions – especially Andrew Anderson, who never stopped pushing – and the entire House Doctor team. Thanks are also due to Jill Brandenburg, Michael Jones and everyone at Harper Collins and Essential Works who helped to create this book.

PICTURE CREDITS

Amtico 73 (centre left, bottom left)

Andrea Cringean 93 (right)

Bill Stephenson 85 (left)

Brume 153 (top)

Chris Ridley 11, 14, 15, 17, 18, 19, 21 (top centre, top right, bottom right), 22, 23, 25, 26 (bottom right), 27, 28, 29, 30, 31, 32, 33, 35, 36, 37, 38, 40, 41, 42, 43, 44, 45 (bottom), 47 (bottom), 49, 50, 51, 52, 53 (bottom), 54, (top left, bottom centre), 55 (top left), 56, 57, 61, 74, 75, 76, 77 (right), 80, 81, 84 (top left, bottom left, bottom right), 88, 89, 91, 98, 101 (top right, bottom right), 111, 112 (top left, bottom left, bottom right), 113 (top left), 116, 117, 119 (top), 121, 126, 127, 130, 132, 133 (bottom), 134, 135 (top), 138, 139 (top), 140, 157 (right)

Christopher Wray Lighting 108, 109

Clyde Combustions Ltd 135 (bottom)

Crown Decorative Products 26 (bottom left), 54 (bottom right), 68 (left), 69 (bottom), 82, 85 (centre), 92 (bottom centre, bottom right), 100 (bottom right), 101 (centre), 110, 112 (bottom centre), 113 (right), 125

Crown Paints 106, 150 (top)

Dave Young 69 (top), 92 (bottom left), 97, 114, 115, 120, 131 (top), 145 (top), 158 (right)

Glynn Slattery 84 (bottom centre)

H. Lewis/Living Etc/IPC Syndication 86, 87

Hillarys 45 (top)

The Holding Company 143

IKEA 66, 67

Jill Brandenburg 94, 95

Joe Pugliese 83

Lee Hind/Living Etc/IPC Syndication 62, 63 (top left, bottom left, bottom right)

Marble Hill Fireplaces 68 (right)

Marshall Tufflex Window Systems 155, 156 (bottom)

Michelle Jones 26 (top left), 55 (centre), 64, 92 (top left), 93 (centre), 101 (top left)

Natural Flooring Direct 73 (top)

N. Mersh/Living Etc/IPC Syndication 107, 123

Nikki English 6, 65, 99, 141

The Pier 148

Robert Harding 96, 118, 139 (bottom), 150 (bottom), 154

Scott Del Amo/Cobra Ltd 131 (bottom), 133 (top)

Sian Trenberth 13, 20 (centre), 55 (right)

Simon Whitmore/Living Etc/IPC Syndication 18, 47 (top)

Stuart Chorley 20 (left), 26 (bottom centre), 54 (bottom left), 90, 93 (left), 100 (top, bottom left), 113 (top centre)

T. Young/Living Etc/IPC Syndication 63 (top right), 104, 105, 159

World's End Tiles 73 (bottom right)

All other photographs courtesy of Talkback/Channel 5